125 BEST QUICK BREAD

RECIPES

Robert **ROSE**

125 Best Quick Bread Recipes

Text copyright © 2002 Donna Washburn and Heather Butt

Photographs copyright © 2002 Robert Rose Inc.

For complete cataloguing information, see page 4.

DESIGN, EDITORIAL AND PRODUCTION:	MATTHEWS COMMUNICATIONS DESIGN INC.
PHOTOGRAPHY:	MARK T. SHAPIRO
ART DIRECTION/FOOD PHOTOGRAPHY:	SHARON MATTHEWS
FOOD STYLIST:	KATE BUSH
PROP STYLIST:	CHARLENE ERRICSON
MANAGING EDITOR:	PETER MATTHEWS
INDEXER:	BARBARA SCHON

We acknowledge the financial support of the Government of Canada through the Book Publishing Industry Development Program (BPIDP) for our publishing activities.

Published by: Robert Rose Inc. • 120 Eglinton Ave. E, Suite 1000
Toronto, Ontario, Canada M4P 1E2   Tel: (416) 322-6552

Printed in Canada

1234567 BP 05 04 03 02

Contents

National Library of Canada Cataloguing in Publication Data

Washburn, Donna
    125 best quick bread recipes

Includes index.
ISBN 0-7788-0044-X

      1. Bread. I. Butt, Heather II. Title. III. Title: One hundred
twenty-five best quick bread recipes.

TX769.W375 2002   641.8'15   C2001-903480-6

We dedicate this book
to those who embrace
baking as a family tradition,
who modify recipes to make
them their own and who,
for their own enjoyment,
pass on to the next
generation their
appreciation and
understanding of the
baking tradition.

ACKNOWLEDGEMENTS

Many people have lent a helping hand in making this book a reality. We would like to thank each and every one.

Our thanks to the following suppliers of food products: Jim Coles, Robin Hood Multifoods, for all-purpose and whole wheat flour; the California Walnut Commission, for walnuts and information; Wendi Hiebert, The Ontario Egg Producers, for eggs; and Dennis Gilliam, Bobs Red Mill, for the gluten-free flours. Our special thanks, as well, to those who baked, taste-tested and/or advised us on our gluten free recipes – Carol Coulter, Alexandra Innes, Susan Crapper, Debra Rice and Rita Purcell. Our appreciation also to George J. Hilley for checking the shelves of American supermarkets and providing answers to product questions.

Thank you to the many manufacturers of bread machines who supplied the latest models to our test kitchen: Philips Electronics Ltd.; Proctor Silex/Hamilton Beach; GE; Toastmaster; Breadman; Black and Decker; and Charlescraft. We also appreciate the assistance of Carol Letourneau, Sales Supervisor at the Bay in Kingston, Ontario.

A special thanks goes to Jean Hill, Marketing Coordinator, Food & Beverage/Home Environment Care, Philips Electronics Ltd. Canada (which supplied waffle irons and bread machines), for her continuing assistance and support.

For the wonderful photography that makes our quick breads look good enough to eat right off the page, we want to express our appreciation for the dedication and hard work of Mark T. Shapiro, of Mark Shapiro Photography; food stylist Kate Bush; art director, food photography, Sharon Matthews; and prop stylist Charlene Ericson. Thanks you for performing your special magic to make our quick breads look as appetizing as the breads in our last two cookbooks. Once again, we enjoyed baking the quick breads for the photo shoot.

Bob Dees and his staff, Marian and Arden, at Robert Rose Inc. deserve special thanks for recognizing how we love to bake and for believing in our ability to author a book on quick breads.

Also to Peter Matthews and staff of Matthews Communications Design Inc. for once again taking our work through the editorial, design, layout and production to create such a beautiful book. Peter, you are rapidly becoming our favorite editor. Thank you, Peter – you certainly do have a way with words and make it seem so easy.

A special thank you goes to our families – husbands, sons, daughters-in-law and grandsons – just for continuing to always be there for us. You are the reasons we work hard and have the inner strength to continue on through the difficult times.

And finally, to our readers and fellow bakers: We hope you have as many enjoyable hours baking – or just reading our books – as we have had working to develop the recipes for you.

INTRODUCTION

When our publisher first approached us about developing quick bread recipes for this book, we were overwhelmed by the sheer number of choices. After all, what are quick breads? Well, they offer the same fresh-from-the-oven flavor as traditional yeast breads, and don't require a lot of preparation and baking time. But that's where the similarities end. Quick breads can include everything from savory breads to sweet loaves, from biscuits to pancakes – suitable for serving at breakfast, lunch or dinner. Our challenge was to come up with a selection of recipes that explored all these wonderfully flavorful possibilities.

Our savory selections include breads that incorporate a wide selection of seasonal ingredients (try our BACON 'N' TOMATO HERB LOAF [page 15] or BROCCOLI CHEDDAR CORNBREAD [page 16]), as well as international favorites, such as MEDITERRANEAN LOAF (page 32) or RUSSIAN BLINI (page 33). Another chapter is devoted to quick breads that feature hearty and healthy combinations of grains and nuts, such as PARMESAN WALNUT BREAD (page 42) and WILD RICE AND CRANBERRY LOAF (page 52). All of these breads are delicious on their own or as a complement to a bowl of hot soup, a crisp salad or a hearty stew.

For many people (ourselves included), the term "quick breads" is synonymous with sweet loaves – taken hot from the oven and cooled overnight to increase their moisture for easier slicing. (At least, that's the traditional rationale; we suspect the "overnight" rule may have been invented just to ensure that some would be left for the next day!) And certainly a book like this one would be incomplete without recipes for sweet loaves such as BANANA CHOCOLATE CHIP COFFEE CAKE (page 69) or PRUNE AND APRICOT BREAD (page 111).

We have also included recipes for biscuits, cobblers, crêpes, waffles and pancakes. The quick and easy basics are here, including CHEDDAR DILL BISCUITS (page 55) and BUTTERMILK WAFFLES (page 85), but we have developed new flavors just for you. Try the FRESH TOMATO BASIL DROP BISCUITS (page 59) or the THREE-FRUIT COBBLER (page 64). Both will quickly become family favorites.

If you're watching your diet, you can still enjoy the great flavor of quick breads. Here you'll find fat-reduced recipes such as LOW-FAT APPLESAUCE RAISIN BREAD (page 117). And for all the people who are looking for gluten-free bread recipes (and judging from all the calls and enquiries posted on our website, there are many of you), we've written a special chapter with gluten-free versions of some of our favorite quick breads. We've discovered that their texture, flavor and nutritive value often exceeds that of the "white flour" originals. Even if your diet isn't restricted, they're worth a try.

For those of you who know us from our previous bread machine baking books, we've adapted many of the flavors from those cookbooks for these easy-to-prepare breads. In fact, you might recognize some of the names and flavor combinations, such as our BREAD MACHINE COUNTRY HARVEST QUICK BREAD (page 158). These recipes are specially designed to take advantage of the "quick bread cycle" now featured on many bread machines.

Finally, we've dedicated a chapter to traditional quick breads. (After all, tradition is such an important part of baking!) And here we revisit some of the loaves and biscuits that we remember enjoying so much on visits to our grandmothers' homes, with updated versions of BANANA BREAD (page 169), so fragrant and crunchy with walnuts; LEMON LOAF WITH LEMON GLAZE (page 172), almost soggy with its luscious lemon glaze; thick slices of DATE NUT BREAD (page 170), dark and sweet, spread with butter; and, of course, ZUCCHINI BREAD (page 175), a harvest-time classic.

We continue to be delighted by all the people who tell us how much they love the recipes in our bread machine cookbooks. And we hope you'll enjoy this collection of recipes just as much. We created them just for you – our fellow bakers!

Donna and Heather

About the Recipes

Baked goods are basically created from mixtures of flour and liquid which, depending on the type of product (for example, whether it's a quick bread, cake or yeast bread) are described as "batters" and "doughs."

A batter contains more sugar, fat and liquid than a dough, and bakes into a softer, more tender product, with a finer crumb. Batters can be thin enough to pour (cakes) or so thick that they must be scraped from a bowl with a spatula (quick breads) – or, thicker still, that they are dropped from a spoon (cobblers and muffins). A dough on the other hand, is stiff enough to handle, whether to knead or to roll out. Depending on how it is handled and the specific ingredients used, a dough can be tender enough to flake (pastry) or stiff enough to knead, whether gently (biscuits) or vigorously (yeast breads).

Mixing Techniques

Each baked product is put together by a different method, using a different balance of ingredients. This is why the final results vary so much in appearance and texture. It is important to follow the mixing techniques as given in the quick bread recipes. Each term – including "beat,"

"blend," "combine," "cream," "cut in," "fold" and "knead" – has a specific meaning. If you wish to refresh your memory about any of these terms, their definitions can be found in the Techniques Glossary, pages 183 to 185.

Choosing your Baking Pans

We recommend using shiny metal pans made from aluminum or tin. These reflect heat away from the baked product so that it browns evenly, but not too quickly. Insulated pans require extra baking time to brown, while foods baked in dark-colored pans brown more quickly, requiring less baking time.

Glass baking dishes conduct and retain heat, resulting in thicker, darker crusts. If you use this type, reduce the baking temperature by about 25° F (20° C). For example, if the recipe says to bake at 350° F (180° C), reduce the oven temperature to 325° F (160° C).

Similarly, we have found that metal baking pans with a nonstick finish also require a lower baking temperature. When recipes were baked at the standard 350° F (180° C), the crusts were darker and thicker. The loaves browned too quickly and were frequently burnt by the time the centers

PAN SIZES AND BAKING TIMES

Pan type	Pan size	Quantity of batter used (approx.)	Baking time at 350° F (180° C) (approx.)
Loaf	9- by 5- by 3-inch (2 L)	4 cups (1 L)	70 to 80 minutes
Loaf	8- by 4- by 3-inch (1.5 L)	4 cups (1 L)	50 to 60 minutes
Loaf	7 1/2- by 3 1/2- by 2 1/2-inch (1 L)	4 cups (1 L)	40 to 50 minutes
Mini-loaf	5 3/4- by 3 1/4- by 2 1/2-inch (500 mL)	1 cup (250 mL)	35 to 45 minutes
Mini-loaf	4 1/2- by 2 1/2- by 1 1/2-inch (250 mL)	1 cup (250 mL)	30 to 40 minutes
Muffin cups	2 1/2-inch (7 cm)	1/4 cup (50 mL)	15 to 20 minutes (at 375° F [190° C])
Bundt	10-inch (3 L)	7 cups (1.75 L)	70 to 80 minutes
Springform	10-inch (3 L)	6 cups (1.5 L)	70 to 80 minutes
Square pan	9-inch (2.5 L)	4 cups (1 L)	55 to 65 minutes
Square pan	8-inch (2 L)	4 cups (1 L)	45 to 55 minutes

were baked. So be sure you know what type of pan you have and adjust your oven temperature accordingly.

For best results, it is important to use the size of pan specifically called for in the recipe. We tested and baked all our quick bread recipes in 9- by 5-inch (2 L) loaf pans. Most bake in 8- by 4-inch (1.5 L) pans as well. Just be sure you only fill the pan about three-quarters full. This allows baked goods to bake evenly and prevents batter from overflowing the pan. As a rule, thicker batters rise less than thinner batters. So the thicker the batter, the fuller the pan can be.

If you have a small amount of batter left over, use it to bake one or two muffins. Fill the remaining empty muffin cups with about 1/4 inch (5 mm) water. Be careful when removing the muffin tin from the oven: The water will be hot. Bake muffins at 375° F (190° C).

When checking the size of the pan, measure from the top inside edge to the opposite inside edge. If in doubt, choose a slightly larger pan over one that may be too small.

Before you start to measure and combine your ingredients, prepare your baking pan to prevent the batter from sticking. Either spray the bottom and sides of the baking pan with a nonstick cooking spray or apply vegetable oil with a pastry brush or with a crumpled-up piece of waxed paper.

USING YOUR OVEN

Preheating

Set the oven to the correct temperature when you begin to assemble your ingredients for baking. Most ovens take 10 to 15 minutes to preheat. A preheated oven ensures more even baking. If the product is put in the oven before it has reached the set temperature, it may burn on the top or the bottom before the interior is completely baked.

Placing pans in the oven

To ensure that quick breads bake evenly, it is essential that air circulates freely around the pan (or pans) in the oven. So be sure to place the pans carefully. One pan should be placed on the rack in the center position of the oven. (In fact, unless a recipe states otherwise, you should always use the middle rack.) Two pans can be placed side by side, provided there is a minimum of 1 inch (2.5 cm) between the pans and between the pans and the oven walls. If you are baking 3 or 4 pans at a time, their positions should be staggered on two racks so that no pan is directly under or over the other. The racks should divide the oven in thirds.

Another way to ensure even browning and baking is to rotate the pans between the racks, and back to front, when half the baking time is complete.

Tube pans, large springform and bundt pans should be placed in the lower third of the oven.

Testing for doneness

To avoid loaves that are overbaked and dry, check for doneness at the minimum baking time, then at 3- or 5-minute intervals, using any of the following methods.

The most common is to test with a long wooden or metal skewer inserted in the center of the loaf. It should be free from crumbs and moisture, although there may be exceptions. For example, we often find loaves that contain a lot of moist fruits – such as blueberries and cranberries – may leave the skewer a bit sticky, even though the loaf is done. Similarly, fully baked loaves containing chocolate or other flavored chips may (depending on the size of the chips) leave a residue of melted chocolate on the tester.

A second testing method is similar to that used for testing the doneness of cakes: Gently press the top of the loaf with your fingertips; it should spring back and not show the mark of your finger. Also, the loaf should have *just* started to pull away from the sides of the pan. If it has pulled away too much, the loaf is overbaked and will be dry.

A third test is to use an instant-read thermometer. Insert it at least 2 inches (5 cm) into the quick bread. The thermometer should register 210° F (100° C). Gluten-free breads may be baked to a slightly lower temperature.

Baking is a science as well as an art. So it's important to use the right ingredients and to measure them accurately. Let's take a look at the elements that make up the "science" of quick breads.

FLOUR

The cell structure for every quick bread is provided by flour. Here you can use either all-purpose or cake-and-pastry flour, both of which contain less gluten and more starch than bread flour, yielding a more tender product.

While all-purpose and cake-and-pastry flour create equally good results, you may need to adjust the amount used in our recipes, all of which were developed using all-purpose flour. Use the chart below as a guide. You may find you have to make small adjustments to the amounts shown.

ALL-PURPOSE FLOUR CALLED FOR IN RECIPE	EQUIVALENT AMOUNT OF CAKE-AND-PASTRY FLOUR
1 3/4 cups (425 mL)	2 cups (500 mL)
2 cups (500 mL)	2 1/4 cups (550 mL)
2 1/4 cups (550 mL)	2 1/3 cups (575 mL)

We chose all-purpose flour when developing our recipes, since it is readily available and is often the only flour many bakers keep in their kitchens. Keep in mind, however, that recipes using all-purpose flour are more prone to overmixing (which toughens the loaf), so mix a little less than you might think necessary – just enough so that the ingredients are moistened.

How to store flour. Keep flour in an airtight container in a cool, dry place. Do not store flour in the refrigerator, since it picks up moisture. If storing for longer than 6 months, flour should be frozen in an airtight container. Allow flour to return to room temperature before using.

LIQUIDS

Buttermilk, sour cream and *yogurt* are frequently used in quick bread recipes. They provide addi-tional flavor and improve the keeping quality of the loaves.

Buttermilk and *sour milk* can be used inter-changeably, cup for cup, in recipes. Despite its name, sour milk is not milk that has "gone bad," but milk that is soured with lemon juice or vine-gar. The name "buttermilk" is also misleading, since it is actually low in fat and calories. Buttermilk contains only 2 g fat and 105 calories per 1 cup (250 mL). (Skim or nonfat milk has 90 calories and 0.3 g fat per 1 cup [250 mL].) Buttermilk intensifies flavors such as chocolate and buckwheat, while giving a warm, rich texture to pancakes and biscuits. Buttermilk can be frozen for up to 3 months before it loses flavor. Dry buttermilk powder can be kept for 2 years. Do not reconstitute powdered buttermilk with water before using, since it tends to lump unless whisked well; instead, combine it with other dry ingredients before adding liquid.

And if you can't find any buttermilk? Just substitute an equal amount of plain yogurt.

Fluid milk can be any type you prefer. Whole and 2% milk give a slightly more tender loaf, but 1%, low-fat or skim also work well. Nonfat dry or pow-dered skim milk mixed with water can replace milk. Use 1/4 to 1/3 cup (50 to 75 mL) nonfat dry or skim milk powder mixed in 1 cup (250 mL) water for every 1 cup (250 mL) milk in the recipe.

Fruit juice is a frequently called-for liquid ingredi-ent in our recipes, since it intensifies the flavor of the bread. We prefer thawed frozen concentrated orange and apple juice for even stronger flavors. Purchase unsweetened fruit juices (not fruit "drinks") and read the labels carefully: some con-tain extra sugar and salt which can spoil the flavor balance of the recipe.

Evaporated milk is milk that has 60% of the water removed. If you want to reduce the amount of fat, substitute evaporated low-fat or evaporated skim milk. If a recipe calls for evaporated milk, don't try to substitute fresh milk. (On the other hand, a half-and-half mixture of water and evaporated milk can be substituted for fresh milk.)

Salt

Salt is the world's most widely used seasoning, no doubt because it has a unique ability to intensify the flavors of food. While we minimize the salt in our recipes (so as not to overpower the flavors of fresh herbs and spices), eliminating the salt entirely can make quick breads taste flat. Still, you can cut the salt if you wish; unlike yeast breads, quick breads do not require salt in order to create the right texture.

Leaveners

In quick breads, leaveners are needed to produce carbon dioxide which, when heated, expands the cell-wall structure of the product, resulting in a light, even texture. (Yeast performs this function in yeast breads.) Without a leavening agent, baked goods turn out heavy and dense. Two common leaveners in quick breads are baking soda and baking powder. Both begin to produce carbon dioxide as soon they come into contact with liquids, so the batter must be baked immediately or placed in the refrigerator to slow down the action.

Baking soda is used as a leavening agent in cakes, quick breads and biscuits that contain acidic ingredients such as buttermilk, lemon juice and molasses. Many recipes call for 1/4 tsp (1 mL) baking soda per 1 cup (250 mL) flour used, but this varies widely. If quick breads have a bitter aftertaste, try reducing the amount of baking soda slightly. Baking soda can be kept in your cupboard for 6 months. To test if it is still active, stir 1/4 tsp (1 mL) into 2 tbsp (25 mL) vinegar. If it bubbles rapidly, it is fine to use; otherwise replace it with fresh. Buy only what you expect to use in 6 months.

Baking powder combines baking soda with an acidic ingredient (typically cream of tartar) that activates it to produce carbon dioxide. Many recipes call for 1 tsp (5 mL) baking powder per 1 cup (250 mL) flour, but this ratio varies widely. Baking powder can be kept in your cupboard for up to 6 months. To test if it is still active, stir 1 tsp (5 mL) into 1/3 cup (75 mL) hot water. If it bubbles, it is fine to use. If not, replace it. Baking powder usually has an expiry date on bottom of the package. The recipes in this book were developed using single-acting baking powder. (See Ingredient Glossary, page 177, for a more complete description of the difference between single- and double-acting baking powder.

Cream of tartar is a white crystalline powder used as the acid component of the leavening agent in baking powder. It gives volume and stability to beaten egg whites.

Tips for Successful Quick Bread Baking

- Read the recipe before you begin, and make sure you have all the ingredients.
- Take time to preheat the oven and prepare the pan according to the recipe. Do this before you measure and mix.
- Prepare all ingredients before mixing. This includes zesting lemons, snipping herbs and grating cheese. Use a zester for long thin strips of orange and lemon peel or a fine grater for a more even flavor; the choice is yours. Where a recipe recommends a specific size or shape for an ingredient, it is important to the success of the recipe; follow the instructions precisely.
- Prepare recipes using either all-metric or all-imperial measures. Don't switch back and forth. Measure all ingredients carefully before you begin mixing. Use the correct dry and liquid measures. Measuring just a bit too much or too little can make a big difference.
- Because flour packs down as it sits in the container or bag, stir before measuring it with dry ingredient measures. Spoon the flour lightly into the correct size measure, heap, then level with a metal spatula or the flat back of a knife.
- Check that ingredients are not too cold. Many recipes recommend that they be warmed to room temperature.
- Stir all flours, sugar, leaveners and seasonings together before adding liquids. This ensures even distribution within the finished product.
- Sieve any lumps out of baking powder, baking soda or unsweetened cocoa before measuring. Use a fork to break up any lumps in brown sugar.

- Unless a recipe specifies otherwise, stir all fruits into the dry ingredients to coat with flour before adding liquids. The fruit is then less likely to sink to the bottom.

- Follow mixing instructions carefully. Mix until moist, but not smooth. Overmixing a quick bread results in a less tender loaf.

- Check for doneness at the shorter recommended baking time.

- As a general rule, when doubling a recipe, only add one-and-a-half times the baking soda, baking powder, salt and spices. Don't try to triple a recipe; in our experience, the result is usually a disaster!

TROUBLESHOOTING GUIDE

Sometimes, even with our best efforts, a recipe can yield disappointing results. The difference between success and failure may be in the amount of of leavener used, or some other combination of factors. Use the guide below to help you identify what may have gone wrong and what steps you can take to remedy the situation.

Bread cracks along top center. This is normal for quick bread, since the gas produced by the baking powder is released quickly during baking, causing the newly formed crust to split. If too pronounced, and the loaf tastes dry, you may have a used bit too much flour. Sometimes a huge crack can be eliminated by letting batter sit in the pan at room temperature for 15 to 20 minutes before baking. Don't let it sit longer or the loaf will be short.

Bread has a sunken top. This usually occurs when you have not used enough flour for the amount of liquid. Sometimes too much fat in the recipe produces the same result.

Bread is too dry. Most often this is the result of using too much flour and/or measuring flour that has packed down. Be sure to stir the flour with a spoon before measuring, then spoon lightly into the correct-size dry ingredient measure, heap and level with a straight edge. Check to be sure you are using the correct type of flour – either cake-and-pastry or all-purpose flour – as well as the correct amount for that type. Check the conversion chart (page 10) if in doubt. Overmixing can be another cause: even the slightest amount toughens and dries the loaf. The batter should be lumpy but without any of the dry ingredients visible.

Bread dries out quickly after baking. Loaves that don't contain a lot of fat will dry out faster than those that do. In many of our recipes, we've replaced the fat with fruit purées, which add moisture and act as a preservative. Still, they can dry out faster than higher-fat loaves. To minimize drying, wrap the loaf (after it has cooled completely) or keep it in an airtight container.

Texture is tough. With low-fat breads, this is a common problem. (The price we pay for being healthy!) It is the fat which produces tenderness in quick breads. In addition, with higher-fat ingredients such as shortening or butter, you use a "creaming" method, which allows you to incorporate air and blend ingredients before adding the flour. When using oil and mixing with the "muffin" method (that is, where liquids and dry ingredients are combined separately and then mixed together with a minimum of strokes), it is easier to overmix. A few extra strokes and the product can be tough. You can substitute butter, margarine or shortening for oil in any recipe, and use the creaming method, but you'll increase the cholesterol.

Acid taste. Chances are you used too much baking powder or baking soda. Simply forgetting to level off the measuring spoon could account for this.

Soapy aftertaste. You probably used too much baking soda. Make sure it was the teaspoon measure you used – not the tablespoon! Also check that there are no lumps in the baking soda.

Quick Breads for Every Season

Every season brings its own rewards – whether in the bounty of fresh produce from local farmers' markets or in the joyful gathering of family and friends over the holidays. Here are breads that will create memories throughout the year and for generations to come.

Although North Americans enjoy an abundance of produce throughout the year, we celebrate each season with the foods of its harvest. Our childhood favorites are remembered and, while often served in different ways, still relished.

With springtime the cold and dark of winter gives way to longer days and warmer breezes. The world becomes greener – and promises the seasonal flavors of fresh rhubarb, asparagus and strawberries.

Spring quickly turns into the hot, hazy days of summer, bringing with it fresh herbs, vine-ripened tomatoes and lots of zucchini. Vegetables are plentiful, ready to be used in breads to accompany barbecues and salads. Plums, peaches, apricots and pears – such abundance. Who could not enjoy summer?

But all too soon, the leaves turn gold, orange, russet and red. Autumn harvest colors are reflected in squash, pumpkin and crisp apples. We plan our meals around them and bake them into breads and coffee cakes. Thanksgiving brings family home to enjoy the treats made from the year's harvest.

We return to baking as autumn changes to winter, with its long, cold nights and short, snowy days. The aroma of holiday baking greets us – cranberries, eggnog and rich, sweet baked treats.

TIPS FOR BUYING FRESH PRODUCE

Select fresh, blemish-free produce of high quality and store properly until use. All fruit should be plump, firm and free from blemishes and soft spots. Store fruit unwashed in the refrigerator for 3 to 5 days, but wash well before using.

Choose small light-green or yellow-flaked zucchini that are firm to the touch. Store in an open plastic bag in the refrigerator. Use within a week. When well washed, there's no need to peel.

We bake with beefsteak tomatoes in the summer, chopping them into large chunks, leaving the seeds and peel. In the winter, a firmer-fleshed tomato (such as Roma) yields a better flavor.

USING FRESH HERBS

Fragrant and flavorful, fresh herbs enhance any savory quick bread. Pick herbs at their peak – before flowers form and the flavor weakens and becomes bitter. Picking regularly encourages new growth. Fresh herbs can be judged by appearance. Look for deep colors, fresh-looking leaves and stems, while avoiding brown spots, sunburn and pest damage.

If fresh herbs are unavailable, use one-third the amount of dried herbs. To intensify the flavor, crush the leaves in the palm of your hand before using.

Bacon 'n' Tomato Herb Loaf

MAKES 1 LOAF

This bread gives you all the great flavor of a BLT sandwich – without the lettuce, of course! Bake just before lunch so you can serve it warm from the oven.

TIP

Choose firm, meaty tomatoes, such as Italian plum or Roma; they hold their shape well.

Be sure to use real mayonnaise (not whipped salad dressing) for this recipe.

VARIATION

If you can't find fresh oregano and parsley, use one-third the quantity of dried. Basil, thyme, or marjoram can be substituted for the oregano.

Try this recipe with 1/4 cup (50 mL) finely chopped, cooked smoked ham instead of the crumbled bacon.

PREHEAT OVEN TO 350° F (180° C)
9- BY 5-INCH (2 L) LOAF PAN, LIGHTLY GREASED

2 1/2 cups mL	all-purpose flour	625
1 tbsp mL	granulated sugar	15
1 tbsp mL	baking powder	15
1/4 cup mL	snipped fresh oregano	50
2 tbsp mL	snipped fresh parsley	25
8 8	slices crisp bacon, crumbled	
1 cup mL	milk	250
1/2 cup mL	mayonnaise	125
2/3 cup mL	chopped plum tomatoes (Roma variety)	150

1. In a large bowl, stir together flour, sugar, baking powder, oregano and parsley. Stir in bacon.

2. In a separate bowl, using an electric mixer, beat milk and mayonnaise until combined. Pour mixture over dry ingredients and stir just until combined. Fold in tomatoes. Spoon into prepared pan.

3. Bake in preheated oven for 70 to 80 minutes or until a cake tester inserted in the center comes out clean. Let cool in pan on rack for 10 minutes. Remove from pan. Serve warm or cold.

Broccoli Cheddar Cornbread

MAKES NINE 3-INCH (7.5 CM) SQUARE PIECES

This bread is just the thing to have on hand if you're entertaining – just cut into bite-size pieces and serve hot or cold as an hors d'oeuvre. It's great for a family meal too!

TIP

Try baking this cornbread in a 2-quart (2 L) ovenproof glass casserole dish and serve hot, directly from the oven. Reduce oven temperature to 325° F (160° C).

Don't be worried by the skimpy amount of thick batter in this recipe. The bread puffs as it bakes to yield a hearty loaf.

No need to cook the broccoli before adding – just cut into small florets.

For a gluten-free version of this bread, see page 132.

VARIATION

For added convenience, replace the dry ingredients with an 8 1/2-oz (240 g) package of corn-muffin or quick-bread mix.

PREHEAT OVEN TO 350° F (180° C)
9-INCH (2.5 L) SQUARE PAN, LIGHTLY GREASED

3/4 cup	all-purpose flour	175 mL
1/2 cup	cornmeal	125 mL
1/4 cup	granulated sugar	50 mL
2 tbsp	baking powder	25 mL
1/2 tsp	salt	2 mL
1/3 cup	vegetable oil	75 mL
3	eggs	3
1 cup	broccoli florets	250 mL
1 cup	shredded old Cheddar cheese	250 mL
1 cup	finely chopped onions	250 mL

1. In a large bowl, stir together, flour, cornmeal, sugar, baking powder and salt.

2. In a separate bowl, using an electric mixer, beat oil and eggs until combined. Pour mixture over dry ingredients and stir just until combined. Gently fold in broccoli, cheese and onion. Spoon into prepared pan.

3. Bake in preheated oven for 30 to 40 minutes or until a cake tester inserted in the center comes out clean. Serve hot.

Cranberry Zucchini Loaf

MAKES 1 LOAF

PREHEAT OVEN TO 350° F (180° C)

9- BY 5-INCH (2 L) LOAF PAN, LIGHTLY GREASED

2 cups	all-purpose flour	500 mL
3/4 cup	granulated sugar	175 mL
1 tbsp	baking powder	15 mL
1/2 tsp	baking soda	2 mL
1/2 tsp	salt	2 mL
1 tsp	ground cinnamon	5 mL
1/4 tsp	ground nutmeg	1 mL
1 cup	grated zucchini	250 mL
1/3 cup	chopped walnuts	75 mL
1/4 cup	vegetable oil	50 mL
2	eggs	2
1/4 cup	milk	50 mL
1/2 cup	fresh or frozen cranberries	125 mL

Flecks of dark green zucchini contrast beautifully with the deep red cranberries nestled in this loaf. It's a treat for the eyes – and your tastebuds!

TIP

Zucchini is a great low calorie source of niacin, potassium and vitamins A and C.

The batter should be drop-biscuit thick, so resist the urge to add more milk. The zucchini will provide all the moisture you need.

If using frozen cranberries, leave in the freezer until just before using. This will help to prevent them from "bleeding" into the bread.

VARIATION

Try this bread using an equal amount of grated cucumber or carrot for all or part of the zucchini.

1. In a large bowl, stir together flour, sugar, baking powder, baking soda, salt, cinnamon and nutmeg. Stir in zucchini and walnuts.

2. In a separate bowl, using an electric mixer, beat oil, eggs and milk until combined. Pour mixture over dry ingredients and stir just until combined. Gently fold in cranberries. Spoon into prepared pan.

3. Bake in preheated oven for 70 to 80 minutes or until a cake tester inserted in the center comes out clean. Let cool in pan on rack for 10 minutes. Remove from pan and let cool completely on rack.

Fruited Pumpkin Loaf

MAKES 1 LOAF

PREHEAT OVEN TO 350° F (180° C)
9- BY 5-INCH (2 L) LOAF PAN, LIGHTLY GREASED

Combining the sweetness of dates and apricots, this loaf is perfect to serve with fruit and cheese for lunch.

TIP

Be sure to buy pumpkin purée – not pumpkin pie filling, which is too sweet and contains too much moisture for this recipe.

VARIATION

Use 1/2 tsp (2 mL) each cinnamon, cloves, ginger and nutmeg for the pumpkin pie spice.

1 cup	whole wheat flour	250 mL
1 cup	all-purpose flour	250 mL
1/2 cup	packed brown sugar	125 mL
1/2 tsp	baking powder	2 mL
1 tsp	baking soda	5 mL
1/2 tsp	salt	2 mL
1 tbsp	grated orange zest	15 mL
2 tsp	pumpkin pie spice	10 mL
1/2 cup	snipped dried apricots	125 mL
1/2 cup	chopped dates	125 mL
1/2 cup	chopped walnuts	125 mL
1/4 cup	vegetable oil	50 mL
2	eggs	2
1 1/4 cups	canned pumpkin purée (not pie filling)	300 mL
1/2 cup	orange juice	125 mL
2 tbsp	molasses	25 mL

1. In a large bowl, stir together whole wheat flour, flour, brown sugar, baking powder, baking soda, salt, zest and pumpkin pie spice. Stir in dried apricots, dates and walnuts.

2. In a separate bowl, using an electric mixer, beat oil, eggs, pumpkin and orange juice until combined. Add molasses while mixing. Pour mixture over dry ingredients and stir just until combined. Spoon into prepared pan.

3. Bake in preheated oven for 70 to 80 minutes or until a cake tester inserted in the center comes out clean. Let cool in pan on rack for 10 minutes. Remove from pan and let cool completely on rack.

Pizza Quick Bread

MAKES 1 LOAF

Enjoy the zesty flavor of pizza in the shape of a quick bread. For best taste and aroma, be sure to serve this bread warm from the oven.

TIP

Use dry, not oil-packed, sun-dried tomatoes. Snip into small pieces so they distribute evenly throughout the loaf.

If you don't own a kitchen scale, have the pepperoni weighed at the deli counter of the grocery store.

VARIATION

Add 1/3 cup (75 mL) sliced ripe olives.

PREHEAT OVEN TO 350° F (180° C)
9- BY 5-INCH (2 L) LOAF PAN, LIGHTLY GREASED

2 1/4 cups	all-purpose flour	550 mL
2 tsp	baking powder	10 mL
1/2 tsp	baking soda	2 mL
1/4 cup	snipped fresh chives	50 mL
1 tbsp	snipped fresh basil	15 mL
1 tbsp	snipped fresh oregano	15 mL
2	cloves garlic, minced	2
1 1/2 cups	shredded old Cheddar cheese	375 mL
1/3 cup	finely chopped sun-dried tomatoes	75 mL
1 oz	sliced pepperoni, chopped	25 g
1 1/2 cups	buttermilk	375 mL

1. In a large bowl, stir together flour, baking powder, baking soda, chives, basil, oregano and garlic. Stir in cheese, tomatoes, pepperoni and buttermilk. Spoon into prepared pan.

2. Bake in preheated oven for 70 to 80 minutes or until a cake tester inserted in the center comes out clean. Let cool in pan on rack for 10 minutes. Remove from pan. Serve warm.

Provolone, Cornmeal and Sage Loaf

MAKES 1 LOAF

PREHEAT OVEN TO 350° F (180° C)
9- BY 5-INCH (2 L) LOAF PAN, LIGHTLY GREASED

This hot and spicy treat is great for lunch – the perfect accompaniment to chili or soup on a cold winter's day.

TIP

For cheese weight/volume equivalents, see Ingredient Glossary (page 178).

VARIATION

Substitute an equal amount of dried dill for the sage.

Try this recipe with any tangy cheese, such as Asiago or Swiss, instead of the Provolone.

1 1/2 cups	all-purpose flour	375 mL
1 cup	cornmeal	250 mL
2 tsp	baking powder	10 mL
1/2 tsp	baking soda	2 mL
1 tsp	salt	5 mL
1 tsp	rubbed sage	5 mL
3/4 tsp	coarsely ground pepper	4 mL
1/8 tsp	cayenne pepper	0.5 mL
1 cup	shredded Provolone cheese	250 mL
2 tbsp	vegetable oil	25 mL
2	eggs	2
1 1/4 cups	buttermilk	300 mL

1. In a large bowl, stir together flour, cornmeal, baking powder, baking soda, salt, sage, pepper and cayenne. Stir in cheese.

2. In a separate bowl, using an electric mixer, beat oil, eggs and buttermilk. Pour mixture over dry ingredients and stir just until combined. Spoon into prepared pan.

3. Bake in preheated oven for 70 to 80 minutes or until a cake tester inserted in the center comes out clean. Let cool in pan on rack for 10 minutes. Remove from pan. Serve warm.

Tomato Spinach Cornbread

**MAKES NINE 3-INCH
(7.5 CM) SQUARE PIECES**

PREHEAT OVEN TO 350° F (180° C)
9-INCH (2.5 L) SQUARE PAN, LIGHTLY GREASED

*Served cold or hot, this
bread is ideal for a
summer luncheon.*

TIP

Choose a beefsteak or
another juicy type of tomato, cut into large chunks.

Be sure to wash and dry
spinach well before packing
into the measuring cup.

VARIATION

For added convenience,
replace the dry ingredients
with an 8 1/2-oz (240 g)
package of corn-muffin
or quick-bread mix.

3/4 cup	all-purpose flour	175 mL
1/2 cup	cornmeal	125 mL
2 tbsp	granulated sugar	25 mL
2 tbsp	baking powder	25 mL
1/2 tsp	salt	2 mL
2 tbsp	snipped fresh oregano	25 mL
1/4 cup	olive oil	50 mL
4	eggs	4
1 1/2 cups	packed chopped fresh spinach	375 mL
1 1/2 cups	coarsely chopped tomatoes	375 mL
1 tbsp	dried minced onion	15 mL

1. In a large bowl, stir together, flour, cornmeal, sugar,
baking powder, salt and oregano.

2. In a separate bowl, using an electric mixer, beat oil and
eggs until combined. Pour mixture over dry ingredients
and stir just until combined. Gently fold in spinach,
tomatoes and onion. Spoon into prepared pan.

3. Bake in preheated oven for 30 to 40 minutes or until a
cake tester inserted in the center comes out clean.
Serve hot.

Rhubarb Orange Bread

MAKES 1 LOAF

PREHEAT OVEN TO 350° F (180° C)
9- BY 5-INCH (2 L) LOAF PAN, LIGHTLY GREASED

Looking for a new way to enjoy the first fruit of the spring harvest? Try this soft, slightly sweet loaf.

TIP

The rhubarb must be finely chopped; otherwise, the finished loaf tends to crumble when sliced.

VARIATION

Substitute pecans or pistachios for the walnuts and lemon zest for the orange.

1 3/4 cups	finely chopped rhubarb	425 mL
1/3 cup	granulated sugar	75 mL
2 cups	all-purpose flour	500 mL
2 tsp	baking powder	10 mL
3/4 tsp	baking soda	4 mL
1/2 tsp	salt	2 mL
2 tbsp	grated orange zest	25 mL
1/2 cup	chopped walnuts	125 mL
3 tbsp	vegetable oil	45 mL
1	egg	1
2/3 cup	orange juice	150 mL
1 tsp	vanilla extract	5 mL

1. In a bowl combine rhubarb and sugar; set aside for 10 to 15 minutes.

2. In a large bowl, stir together flour, baking powder, baking soda, salt and zest. Stir in walnuts.

3. In a separate bowl, using an electric mixer, beat oil, egg, juice and vanilla extract until combined. Stir in reserved rhubarb mixture. Pour over dry ingredients and stir just until combined. Spoon into prepared pan.

4. Bake in preheated oven for 70 to 80 minutes or until a cake tester inserted in the center comes out clean. Let cool in pan on rack for 10 minutes. Remove from pan and let cool completely on rack.

Peach Blueberry Quick Bread

MAKES 1 LOAF

As pleasing to the eye as it is to the palate, this attractive quick bread makes a sweet treat to serve in summer, at the height of peach and blueberry season.

TIP

If using frozen blueberries, leave in the freezer until just before using. This will help to prevent them from "bleeding" into the bread.

VARIATION

For a milder spice flavor, use mace or nutmeg instead of the cardamom.

Substitute plums for the blueberries.

PREHEAT OVEN TO 350° F (180° C)
9- BY 5-INCH (2 L) LOAF PAN, LIGHTLY GREASED

1 3/4 cups	all-purpose flour	425 mL
2 1/2 tsp	baking powder	12 mL
3/4 tsp	salt	4 mL
1/2 tsp	ground cardamom	2 mL
1/3 cup	shortening	75 mL
2/3 cup	granulated sugar	150 mL
2	eggs	2
1/3 cup	milk	75 mL
1 cup	chopped fresh peaches	250 mL
1/2 cup	fresh or frozen blueberries	125 mL

1. In a large bowl, stir together flour, baking powder, salt and cardamom.

2. In a separate large bowl, using an electric mixer, cream shortening, sugar and eggs until light and fluffy. Stir in dry ingredients alternately with milk, making 3 additions of dry ingredients and 2 of milk; stir just until combined. Gently fold in peaches and blueberries. Spoon into prepared pan.

3. Bake in preheated oven for 70 to 80 minutes or until a cake tester inserted in the center comes out clean. Let cool in pan on rack for 10 minutes. Remove from pan and let cool completely on rack.

Golden Harvest Loaf

MAKES 1 LOAF

PREHEAT OVEN TO 350° F (180° C)
9- BY 5-INCH (2 L) LOAF PAN, LIGHTLY GREASED

This loaf reminds us of an autumn wheat field ready for harvest.

TIP

Microwave the sweet potato to cook it as you would a regular baking potato. Cook until fork-tender. (Cooking time will depend on the size of the potato.) Mash or chop when cool enough to handle.

VARIATION

Substitute canned sweet potatoes or yams for the fresh variety.

1 cup	whole wheat flour	250 mL
1 cup	all-purpose flour	250 mL
1/4 cup	packed brown sugar	50 mL
1 tbsp	baking powder	15 mL
1/2 tsp	salt	2 mL
3/4 cup	chopped dried apricots	175 mL
1/4 cup	vegetable oil	50 mL
2	eggs	2
1 1/4 cups	cooked sweet potato (See Tip, at left)	300 mL
1/4 cup	maple syrup	50 mL

1. In a large bowl, stir together whole wheat flour, flour, brown sugar, baking powder and salt. Stir in apricots.

2. In a separate bowl, using an electric mixer, beat oil, eggs, sweet potato and maple syrup until combined. Pour mixture over dry ingredients and stir just until combined. Spoon into prepared pan.

3. Bake in preheated oven for 70 to 80 minutes or until a cake tester inserted in the center comes out clean. Let cool in pan on rack for 10 minutes. Remove from pan and let cool completely on rack.

Pumpkin Bran Bread

MAKES 1 LOAF

PREHEAT OVEN TO 350° F (180° C)
9- BY 5-INCH (2 L) LOAF PAN, LIGHTLY GREASED

This extra-moist loaf tastes like a bran muffin. Thinly sliced, it makes a perfect breakfast-on-the-run.

TIP

Be sure to buy pumpkin purée – not pumpkin pie filling, which is too sweet and contains too much moisture for this recipe.

VARIATION

Substitute oat bran for wheat bran. Evaporated milk can replace the buttermilk.

1 1/4 cups	whole wheat flour	300 mL
3/4 cup	wheat bran	175 mL
3/4 cup	granulated sugar	175 mL
2 tsp	baking powder	10 mL
1 tsp	baking soda	5 mL
1 tsp	salt	5 mL
1 tsp	ground cinnamon	5 ml
1/2 tsp	ground allspice	2 mL
1/2 tsp	ground nutmeg	2 mL
1 cup	raisins	250 mL
2 tbsp	vegetable oil	25 mL
2	eggs	2
1 cup	canned pumpkin purée (not pie filling)	250 mL
3/4 cup	buttermilk	175 mL

1. In a large bowl, stir together whole wheat flour, wheat bran, sugar, baking powder, baking soda, salt, cinnamon, allspice and nutmeg. Stir in raisins.

2. In a separate bowl, using an electric mixer, beat oil, eggs, pumpkin and buttermilk until combined. Pour mixture over dry ingredients and stir just until combined. Spoon into prepared pan.

3. Bake in preheated oven for 70 to 80 minutes or until a cake tester inserted in the center comes out clean. Let cool in pan on rack for 10 minutes. Remove from pan and let cool completely on rack.

Mock Christmas Cake

MAKES 1 LOAF

*Traditional Christmas cakes
are delicious, but need to
be aged well in advance.
Try this quick version when
you're short of time.*

2 cups	mixed dried fruit	500 mL
2 tbsp	brandy	25 mL
1 3/4 cups	all-purpose flour	425 mL
2 tsp	baking powder	10 mL
1/2 tsp	salt	2 mL
1 tbsp	ground cardamom	15 mL
1/3 cup	soft butter	75 mL
1/2 cup	granulated sugar	125 mL
2	eggs	2
3/4 cup	milk	175 mL

TIP

Use any combination of
raisins, dried currants,
glazed cherries, candied
ginger, candied peel,
candied pineapple and
citron.

The longer the fruit soaks,
the stronger the brandy
flavor. Be sure you
don't drain the fruit and
discard the brandy!

VARIATION

Add some nuts to the dried
fruit mixture.

Substitute thawed, frozen
orange or apple juice
concentrate for the brandy.

1. In a small bowl, combine dried fruit and brandy; set aside.

2. In a bowl stir together flour, baking powder, salt and cardamom.

3. In a separate large bowl, using an electric mixer, cream the butter and sugar. Add eggs; cream until light and fluffy. Stir in dry ingredients alternately with milk, making 3 additions of dry ingredients and 2 of milk; stir just until combined after each addition. Fold in dried fruit and brandy mixture. Spoon into prepared pan.

4. Bake in preheated oven for 70 to 80 minutes or until a cake tester inserted in the center comes out clean. Let cool in pan on rack for 10 minutes. Remove from pan and let cool completely on rack.

International

Over the centuries, immigrants have come to North America, bringing with them their recipes and adapting them to New World ingredients, while still evoking the warmth and memories of their homelands. Try these recipes and enjoy the many baking traditions!

North America's food culture has evolved from the many contributions of peoples from around the world. Traditional dishes from other countries, modified to suit the ingredients available in our climate, have become our own.

In this chapter you'll find recipes from the eastern Maritime provinces in Canada, as well as New England in the United States, originally brought to our shores from Scotland. Try the Scottish Oatmeal Scones and Maritime Molasses Date Bran Loaf. Both are perfect served with homemade baked beans — also a traditional dish from this region.

Irish soda bread is another favorite. It comes in two colors (white and brown) and two types ("cake," common in the south of Ireland, and "farl," which comes from the north). In this chapter you'll find our recipe for the whole wheat cake version. Traditionally, this bread was made either "in the pot" or on the "bake stone." The loaf has a cross cut in the top to allow the bread to stretch and expand as it rises. (Farl, on the other hand, is rolled out to a rough circle and cut through crosswise into 4 pieces.) Only the "tea bread" version contains raisins, currants or other fruit.

Blini are of Russian origin. These small, yeast-leavened buckwheat pancakes are traditional fare in many North American households at Thanksgiving and Christmas.

From the Mediterranean region come breads rich in olive oil, sun-dried tomatoes and a rich variety of herbs native to the region.

Enjoy them all!

Fruited Barm Brack

MAKES 1 LOAF

PREHEAT OVEN TO 350° F (180° C)
9- BY 5-INCH (2 L) LOAF PAN, LIGHTLY GREASED

Barm brack, meaning "yeast bread" in Gaelic, is an Irish bread with raisins or currants and candied fruit peel – although it is not always made with yeast. Try our fruited version made with tea, apricots and cranberries.

TIP

Snip dried apricots into 1/4-inch (5 mm) pieces with sharp scissors.

VARIATION

Try replacing one or more of the fruits with an equal quantity of dried cherries, dried apples or fresh dates.

2 cups	all-purpose flour	500 mL
1/2 cup	packed brown sugar	125 mL
2 tsp	baking powder	10 mL
1/2 tsp	baking soda	2 mL
1/2 tsp	salt	2 mL
1 tsp	ground cinnamon	5 mL
1 tsp	ground nutmeg	5 mL
1/2 cup	snipped dried apricots	125 mL
1/2 cup	currants	125 mL
1/2 cup	dried cranberries	125 mL
2 tbsp	vegetable oil	25 mL
1	egg	1
1 cup	tea (at room temperature)	250 mL

1. In a large bowl, stir together flour, brown sugar, baking powder, baking soda, salt, cinnamon and nutmeg. Stir in dried apricots, currants and dried cranberries.

2. In a separate bowl, using an electric mixer, beat oil, egg and tea until combined. Pour mixture over dry ingredients and stir just until combined. Spoon into prepared pan.

3. Bake in preheated oven for 70 to 80 minutes or until a cake tester inserted in the center comes out clean. Let cool in pan on rack for 10 minutes. Remove from pan and let cool completely on rack.

Irish Whole Wheat Soda Bread

MAKES 1 ROUND LOAF

PREHEAT OVEN TO 400° F (200° C)
BAKING SHEET, LIGHTLY GREASED

Like a traditional hearth bread, this loaf features a crusty exterior and soft interior, with a slightly tangy flavor. It's perfect with Irish stew or corned beef and cabbage.

2 cups	whole wheat flour	500 mL
1 cup	all-purpose flour	250 mL
1 tbsp	granulated sugar	15 mL
1 tsp	baking powder	5 mL
1 tsp	baking soda	5 mL
1 tsp	salt	5 mL
1 1/2 cups	buttermilk	375 mL

TIP

Score the top of the round at least 1/2 inch (1 cm) deep. This will ensure it breaks easily into wedges. The cuts for the "cake" should go deeper – half way down through the center of the circle – to allow the loaf to "flower."

VARIATION

For a fruited version of this bread, add 1 cup (250 mL) raisins, currants and/or walnuts to the dry ingredients just before the buttermilk.

To make this "cake" into a "farl" (see page 28 for explanation): Place the dough in a lightly greased cast iron frying pan after forming into a round.

1. In a large bowl, stir together whole wheat flour, flour, sugar, baking powder, baking soda and salt. Add buttermilk all at once, stirring with a fork to make a soft, but slightly sticky dough.

2. With lightly floured hands, form dough into a ball. On a lightly floured surface, knead the dough gently for 8 to 10 times. Pat the dough into a 6-inch (15 cm) thick round, with a slightly flattened top.

3. Place dough on prepared baking sheet. With a shape knife or pizza cutter, score the top in the shape of a cross or large X. Bake in preheated oven for 35 to 45 minutes. Remove from baking sheet onto a cooling rack immediately. Dust top with rice flour. Serve warm from the oven.

Maritime Molasses Date Bran Loaf

MAKES 1 LOAF

PREHEAT OVEN TO 350° F (180° C)
9- BY 5-INCH (2 L) LOAF PAN, LIGHTLY GREASED

If you like the sweet flavor of dates, you'll love this dark double-bran bread. There's a date in every bite!

TIP

Reduce the molasses by 1 tbsp (15 mL) for a milder flavor.

Be sure that bran has almost completely absorbed the buttermilk before adding it to the batter.

VARIATION

Try using raisins instead of dates and sesame seeds instead of flaxseeds.

1 cup	buttermilk	250 mL
2/3 cup	bran cereal	150 mL
2/3 cup	wheat bran	150 mL
1/2 cup	whole wheat flour	125 mL
1 1/4 cups	all-purpose flour	300 mL
1/3 cup	packed brown sugar	75 mL
1 tbsp	baking powder	15 mL
1 1/2 tsp	baking soda	7 mL
1/4 tsp	salt	1 mL
1 cup	chopped dates	250 mL
2 tbsp	flaxseeds	25 mL
1/4 cup	vegetable oil	50 mL
1	egg	1
2/3 cup	molasses	150 mL

1. In a bowl stir together buttermilk, bran cereal and wheat bran; set aside for 10 minutes.

2. In a large bowl, stir together whole wheat flour, flour, brown sugar, baking powder, baking soda and salt. Stir in dates and flaxseeds.

3. In a separate bowl, using an electric mixer, beat oil and egg until combined. Add molasses while mixing. Pour over dry ingredients along with reserved buttermilk/bran mixture; stir just until combined. Spoon into prepared pan.

4. Bake in preheated oven for 70 to 80 minutes or until a cake tester inserted in the center comes out clean. Let cool in pan on rack for 10 minutes. Remove from pan and let cool completely on rack.

Mediterranean Loaf

MAKES 1 LOAF

PREHEAT OVEN TO 350° F (180° C)
9- BY 5-INCH (2 L) LOAF PAN, LIGHTLY GREASED

Be sure to keep a jar of oil-packed sun-dried tomatoes in the cupboard for this recipe. It's a great accompaniment to souvlaki and a Greek salad.

TIP

Make sure the chopped tomatoes are thoroughly separated and coated with the flour mixture before adding the liquid ingredients.

If there isn't enough oil in the jar of tomatoes, add sufficient olive oil to make up the 3 tbsp (45 mL).

VARIATION

Substitute Tilsit, Asiago or another tangy cheese for the feta.

2 cups	all-purpose flour	500 mL
2 tbsp	granulated sugar	25 mL
2 tsp	baking powder	10 mL
1/2 cup	crumbled feta cheese	125 mL
1/2 cup	chopped drained oil-packed sun-dried tomatoes (3 tbsp [45 mL] oil reserved)	125 mL
1/3 cup	sliced ripe olives	75 mL
2 to 3	cloves garlic, minced	2 to 3
3 tbsp	oil reserved from tomatoes (above)	45 mL
2	eggs	2
1 cup	milk	250 mL

1. In a large bowl, stir together flour, sugar and baking powder. Stir in cheese, tomatoes, olives and garlic.

2. In a separate bowl, using an electric mixer, beat oil, eggs and milk until combined. Pour mixture over dry ingredients and stir just until combined. Spoon into prepared pan.

3. Bake in preheated oven for 70 to 80 minutes or until a cake tester inserted in the center comes out clean. Let cool in pan on rack for 10 minutes. Remove from pan and let cool completely on rack.

CHEDDAR DILL BISCUITS (PAGE 55) ➤

Russian Blini

**MAKES EIGHTEEN
2-INCH (5 CM) BLINI**

These little yeast-leavened
buckwheat pancakes
are traditionally served
with sour cream, caviar
and smoked salmon. They
make a wonderful treat for
Thanksgiving or Christmas.

CRÊPE PAN OR FRYPAN, LIGHTLY GREASED

1/3 cup	milk	75 mL
1/2 tsp	granulated sugar	2 mL
1/2 tsp	instant yeast	2 mL
1	egg yolk	1
1 tsp	vegetable oil	5 mL
1/3 cup	all-purpose flour	75 mL
2 tbsp	buckwheat flour	25 ml
1/4 tsp	salt	1 mL
2	egg whites	2
Pinch	cream of tartar	Pinch

TIP

Blini can be prepared in
a frypan, crêpe pan or
on a grill. The choice is
up to you.

For fluffier pancakes,
warm egg whites to room
temperature before using.
(See Techniques
Glossary, page 183.)

For additional tips, see the
introduction to "Crêpes,
Pancakes and Waffles" on
page 84.

VARIATION

For a stronger buckwheat
flavor, increase the buckwheat flour to 3 tbsp
(45 mL) and decrease the
flour to 1/4 cup (50 mL).

1. In a small microwaveable bowl, heat milk to lukewarm.
   Stir in sugar and yeast.

2. In another bowl, whisk together egg yolk and oil. Add
   yeast mixture, flour, buckwheat flour and salt stirring
   until smooth. Cover and set in a pan of warm water for
   1 1/4 hours.

3. In a separate bowl, using an electric mixer, beat egg
   whites and cream of tartar until stiff (but not dry) peaks
   form; using a spatula, fold whites gently into batter.

4. Heat pan until medium hot. Using 2 tbsp (25 mL)
   batter, spoon into hot pan. Spread batter, with the back
   of a spoon, for thinner blini. When the underside is
   brown, turn and cook about 30 to 60 seconds longer
   or until the second side is golden brown. Repeat with
   remaining batter.

◄ ROSEMARY SCONES TOPPED WITH CARAMELIZED VIDALIAS (PAGE 60)

Scottish Oatmeal Scones

**MAKES FOURTEEN
2-INCH (5 CM) SCONES**

Served hot from the oven and drizzled with honey, these oatmeal scones add the perfect homemade touch to any meal.

TIP

To enjoy the next day, split scones in half and reheat in a toaster oven.

See "Tips and Techniques for Tender Biscuits and Scones" (page 54).

VARIATION

For a heavier, more traditional oatmeal biscuit, omit the shortening.

PREHEAT OVEN TO 425° F (220° C)
BAKING SHEET, LIGHTLY GREASED

1 cup	whole wheat flour	250 mL
1 1/4 cups	all-purpose flour	300 mL
1/2 cup	quick-cooking oats	125 mL
2 tsp	baking powder	10 mL
3/4 tsp	salt	4 mL
1/3 cup	shortening	75 mL
1	egg	1
3/4 cup	buttermilk	175 mL

1. In a large bowl, stir together whole wheat flour, flour, oats, baking powder and salt. Using a pastry blender, cut in shortening until mixture resembles coarse crumbs.

2. In a small bowl, whisk together egg and buttermilk. Pour over dry ingredients all at once, stirring with a fork to make a soft, but slightly sticky dough.

3. With lightly floured hands, form dough into a ball. On a lightly floured surface, knead the dough gently for 8 to 10 times. Pat or roll out the dough into a 1-inch (2.5 cm) thick round.

4. Using a 2-inch (5 cm) floured biscuit cutter, cut out as many rounds as possible. Place on baking sheet. Gently form scraps into a ball, flatten and cut out rounds.

5. Bake in preheated oven for 12 to 15 minutes. Remove from baking sheet onto a cooling rack immediately. Serve warm.

Southern Cornbread

MAKES 1 LOAF

Here's a new twist on an old favorite – traditional cornbread enriched with the flavor of two kinds of cheese, and chili peppers to provide a burst of heat.

TIP

For a spicier cornbread, increase the amount of red pepper flakes to taste.

VARIATION

Add 2 or 3 slices of crumbled crisp bacon. You might want to decrease the salt by 1/4 tsp (1 mL).

1 cup	all-purpose flour	250 mL
1 1/4 cups	cornmeal	300 mL
1/2 cup	granulated sugar	125 mL
2 tsp	baking powder	10 mL
1/2 tsp	salt	2 mL
1 tsp	crushed red pepper flakes	5 mL
1 cup	shredded old Cheddar cheese	250 mL
1 cup	shredded Monterey Jack cheese	250 mL
1 cup	thawed frozen corn kernels	250 mL
1/3 cup	vegetable oil	75 mL
2	eggs	2
1 cup	buttermilk	250 mL

1. In a large bowl, stir together flour, cornmeal, sugar, baking powder, salt and pepper flakes. Stir in cheeses and corn.

2. In a separate bowl, using an electric mixer, beat oil, eggs and buttermilk. Pour mixture over dry ingredients and stir just until combined. Spoon into prepared pan.

3. Bake in preheated oven for 70 to 80 minutes or until a cake tester inserted in the center comes out clean. Let cool in pan on rack for 10 minutes. Remove from pan and let cool completely on rack.

Swiss Apple Bread

MAKES 1 LOAF

What do you get when you take the traditional pairing of Swiss cheese and apples, and combine it with the crunch of 7-grain cereal and walnuts? A great mid-morning snack!

TIP

Any type of grain cereal (3-, 5-, 7- or 12-grain) works well in this recipe. Red River cereal is good too.

VARIATION

Add 1 to 2 tbsp (15 to 25 mL) caraway or fennel seeds.

PREHEAT OVEN TO 350° F (180° C)
9- BY 5-INCH (2 L) LOAF PAN, LIGHTLY GREASED

2 cups	all-purpose flour	500 mL
1/3 cup	granulated sugar	75 mL
1 tbsp	baking powder	15 mL
1/2 tsp	salt	2 mL
1 cup	diced apples	250 mL
3/4 cup	shredded Swiss cheese	175 mL
1/2 cup	7-grain cereal	125 mL
1/2 cup	chopped walnuts	125 mL
2 tbsp	vegetable oil	25 mL
2	eggs	2
1/2 cup	frozen apple juice concentrate, thawed	125 mL
1/2 cup	milk	125 mL

1. In a large bowl, stir together flour, sugar, baking powder and salt. Stir in apples, cheese, cereal and walnuts.

2. In a separate bowl, using an electric mixer, beat oil, eggs, apple juice concentrate and milk. Pour mixture over dry ingredients and stir just until combined. Spoon into prepared pan.

3. Bake in preheated oven for 70 to 80 minutes or until a cake tester inserted in the center comes out clean. Let cool in pan on rack for 10 minutes. Remove from pan and let cool completely on rack.

Grains, Seeds and Nuts

T hey're so delicious, it's easy to forget that seeds and nuts make a healthy addition to your diet. Enjoy the extra crunch of these tasty breads at mealtime or as a nutritious snack.

Purchase seeds, nuts and whole grains in small quantities and refrigerate or freeze to prevent the fat they contain from turning rancid. If stored for longer than one month, taste before using.

Medium- or large-flake, regular- or quick-cooking oats produce the best results in recipes that call for rolled oats. Substituting instant oats in the quick breads leaves a wet and compact texture. An equal amount of bulgur can be substituted for cracked wheat and oat bran can be substituted for wheat bran. Multigrain cereals are interchangeable with those containing 3, 5, 7 or 12 grains.

When using nuts, dried fruits and seeds in a quick bread recipe, they should be thoroughly coated with the dry ingredients before liquids are added. This helps to provide more even distribution throughout the loaf. When chopping nuts, keep in mind that if the pieces are too large, they tend to sink to the bottom; if they're too small, you won't get a satisfying crunch.

THE FAT/FIBER CONNECTION

Breads containing seeds and nuts have multiple health benefits. Many contain heart-healthy fats (such as omega-3), as well as fiber and other health-promoting compounds.

Make substitutions based on the list below.

SEEDS (1 cup [250 mL])

	Fat (g)	Fiber (g)
Flaxseed	52	43
Poppy	4	1
Pumpkin	63	5
Sesame	71	17
Sunflower	63	14

NUTS (1 cup [250 mL])

	Fat (g)	Fiber (g)
Almonds	70	15
Hazelnuts (Filberts)	70	11
Macadamia	102	12
Pecans	86	11
Pistachios	55	12
Walnuts	76	4

Carrot Honey Yogurt Bread

MAKES 1 LOAF

PREHEAT OVEN TO 350° F (180° C)
9- BY 5-INCH (2 L) LOAF PAN, LIGHTLY GREASED

Carrots gives this loaf its great color, flavor and texture. What's more, the carrots make the bread even moister on the day after it's baked!

TIP

Shred the carrots just before use, since exposure to air causes them to darken.

VARIATION

Try substituting grated zucchini for all or half the carrots.

For a stronger flavor, increase the amount of nutmeg or try using ground ginger instead.

2 cups	all-purpose flour	500 mL
2 tsp	baking powder	10 mL
1/2 tsp	baking soda	2 mL
1/2 tsp	salt	2 mL
1/4 tsp	ground nutmeg	1 mL
1 1/2 cups	shredded carrots	375 mL
3/4 cup	chopped pecans	175 mL
1/4 cup	vegetable oil	50 mL
1	egg	1
3/4 cup	plain yogurt	175 mL
1/2 cup	honey	125 mL

1. In a large bowl, stir together flour, baking powder, baking soda, salt and nutmeg. Stir in carrots and pecans.

2. In a separate bowl, using an electric mixer, beat oil, egg and yogurt until combined. Add honey while mixing. Pour mixture over dry ingredients and stir just until combined. Spoon into prepared pan.

3. Bake in preheated oven for 70 to 80 minutes or until a cake tester inserted in the center comes out clean. Let cool in pan on rack for 10 minutes. Remove from pan and let cool completely on rack.

Country Harvest Loaf

MAKES 1 LOAF

PREHEAT OVEN TO 350° F (180° C)
9- BY 5-INCH (2 L) LOAF PAN, LIGHTLY GREASED

If you've used our bread machine cookbooks, then chances are this recipe will seem familiar. But since this is one of our all-time favorite flavor combinations, we just had to try a quick bread version. Let us know how you like it!

1 cup	whole wheat flour	250 mL
1 cup	all-purpose flour	250 mL
3/4 cup	packed brown sugar	175 mL
2 tsp	baking powder	10 mL
1 tsp	baking soda	5 mL
1/2 tsp	salt	2 mL
1/4 cup	flaxseeds	50 mL
1/4 cup	sunflower seeds	50 mL
2 tbsp	poppy seeds	25 mL
2 tbsp	sesame seeds	25 mL
1/4 cup	vegetable oil	50 mL
1	egg	1
1 cup	buttermilk	250 mL
1/4 cup	honey	50 mL

TIP

We prefer to use raw, unsalted sunflower seeds for this recipe.

To prevent the seeds from becoming rancid, store in an airtight container in the refrigerator.

VARIATION

Feel free to experiment with different proportions of seeds in this recipe. Just be sure that the total quantity remains constant.

Pumpkin seeds can be substituted for any of the seeds in the recipe.

1. In a large bowl, stir together whole wheat flour, flour, brown sugar, baking powder, baking soda, salt, flaxseeds, sunflower seeds, poppy seeds and sesame seeds.

2. In a separate bowl, using an electric mixer, beat oil, egg and buttermilk until combined. Add honey while mixing. Pour mixture over dry ingredients and stir just until combined. Spoon into prepared pan.

3. Bake in preheated oven for 70 to 80 minutes or until a cake tester inserted in the center comes out clean. Let cool in pan on rack for 10 minutes. Remove from pan and let cool completely on rack.

Cranberry Pistachio Holiday Bread

MAKES 1 LOAF

PREHEAT OVEN TO 350° F (180° C)

9- BY 5-INCH (2 L) LOAF PAN, LIGHTLY GREASED

The colors in this loaf are perfect for the holidays, but you'll want to serve it all year round.

TIP

If using frozen cranberries, leave in the freezer until just before using. This will help to prevent them from "bleeding" into the bread.

Plan ahead and shell pistachios soon after purchasing to avoid wasting time during preparation.

Purchase cranberries when in season and freeze in the original package for making quick breads.

VARIATION

Use your favorite type of marmalade – lemon, orange or 3-fruit.

2 cups	all-purpose flour	500 mL
1/4 cup	granulated sugar	50 mL
1 1/2 tsp	baking powder	7 mL
1/4 tsp	salt	1 mL
1 tsp	ground cardamom	5 mL
1/2 cup	chopped pistachio nuts	125 ml
1/4 cup	vegetable oil	50 mL
1	egg	1
3/4 cup	milk	175 mL
1/3 cup	marmalade	75 mL
1 1/2 cups	fresh or frozen cranberries	375 mL

1. In a large bowl, stir together flour, sugar, baking powder, salt and cardamom. Stir in nuts.

2. In a separate bowl, using an electric mixer, beat oil, egg and milk until combined. Add marmalade while mixing. Pour mixture over dry ingredients and stir just until combined. Gently fold in cranberries. Spoon into prepared pan.

3. Bake in preheated oven for 70 to 80 minutes or until a cake tester inserted in the center comes out clean. Let cool in pan on rack for 10 minutes. Remove from pan and let cool completely on rack.

Parmesan Walnut Bread

MAKES 1 LOAF

PREHEAT OVEN TO 350° F (180° C)
9- BY 5-INCH (2 L) LOAF PAN, LIGHTLY GREASED

Whole wheat flour and walnuts give this crunchy, golden loaf a high fiber content, while the Parmesan cheese gives it a pleasant tang.

TIP

For a spicier flavor, add a small amount of Dijon mustard or Tabasco sauce.

VARIATION

Substitute vegetable oil for the walnut oil.

Use freshly grated Parmesan (not the ready-grated variety) for a stronger cheese flavor.

1 cup	whole wheat flour	250 mL
1 1/2 cups	all-purpose flour	375 mL
2/3 cup	granulated sugar	150 mL
1 tbsp	baking powder	15 mL
1/2 tsp	salt	2 mL
2/3 cup	grated Parmesan cheese	150 mL
2/3 cup	chopped walnuts	150 mL
3 tbsp	walnut oil	45 mL
1 1/2 cups	milk	375 mL

1. In a large bowl, stir together whole wheat flour, flour, sugar, baking powder and salt. Stir in cheese and walnuts.

2. In a separate bowl, using an electric mixer, beat oil and milk until combined. Pour mixture over dry ingredients and stir just until combined. Spoon into prepared pan.

3. Bake in preheated oven for 70 to 80 minutes or until a cake tester inserted in the center comes out clean. Let cool in pan on rack for 10 minutes. Remove from pan and let cool completely on rack.

Peanut Butter Crunch Loaf

MAKES 1 LOAF

PREHEAT OVEN TO 350° F (180° C)
9- BY 5-INCH (2 L) LOAF PAN, LIGHTLY GREASED

*Top this quick bread with
some raspberry jam or
grape jelly for a
special lunchtime treat.*

3/4 cup	whole wheat flour	175 mL
3/4 cup	all-purpose flour	175 mL
1/3 cup	packed brown sugar	75 mL
2 tsp	baking powder	10 mL
1/2 tsp	baking soda	2 mL
1/2 tsp	salt	2 mL
3/4 cup	chopped peanuts	175 mL
1	egg	1
1 cup	milk	250 mL
1/2 cup	peanut butter	125 mL

TIP

Chopping the peanuts
results in a smooth-
textured bread that
slices easily.

VARIATION

For added crunch,
substitute chunky peanut
butter for the smooth.

1. In a large bowl, stir together whole wheat flour, flour, brown sugar, baking powder, baking soda and salt. Stir in peanuts.

2. In a separate bowl, using an electric mixer, beat egg, milk and peanut butter until combined. Pour mixture over dry ingredients and stir just until combined. Spoon into prepared pan.

3. Bake in preheated oven for 70 to 80 minutes or until a cake tester inserted in the center comes out clean. Let cool in pan on rack for 10 minutes. Remove from pan and let cool completely on rack.

Pecan Squash Loaf

MAKES 1 LOAF

PREHEAT OVEN TO 350° F (180° C)
9- BY 5-INCH (2 L) LOAF PAN, LIGHTLY GREASED

The rich, deep golden color of this bread reminds us of a cool, crisp autumn day.

TIP

Use butternut or Hubbard squash for this recipe. Scoop out seeds from the squash and cook in the microwave on High for 3 to 4 minutes per pound (500 g). Mash and use as directed.

For a milder flavor, omit all the spices.

The next time you're having squash for dinner, cook some extra and use it to make this bread the next day.

VARIATION

Substitute pumpkin (canned or cooked fresh) for the squash.

Use your favorite combination of pumpkin pie spices.

Substitute thawed frozen apple juice concentrate for the apple juice.

2 cups	all-purpose flour	500 mL
1/2 cup	packed brown sugar	125 mL
2 tsp	baking powder	10 mL
1 1/2 tsp	baking soda	7 mL
1/2 tsp	salt	2 mL
3/4 tsp	ground ginger	4 mL
3/4 tsp	ground nutmeg	4 mL
1/2 tsp	ground allspice	2 mL
3/4 cup	chopped pecans	175 mL
1/4 cup	vegetable oil	50 mL
2	eggs	2
1 cup	mashed cooked squash (see Tip, at left)	250 mL
1/2 cup	unsweetened apple juice	125 mL

1. In a large bowl, stir together flour, brown sugar, baking powder, baking soda, salt, ginger, nutmeg and allspice. Stir in pecans.

2. In a separate bowl, using an electric mixer, beat oil, eggs, squash and apple juice until combined. Pour mixture over dry ingredients and stir just until combined. Spoon into prepared pan.

3. Bake in preheated oven for 70 to 80 minutes or until a cake tester inserted in the center comes out clean. Let cool in pan on rack for 10 minutes. Remove from pan and let cool completely on rack.

Pineapple Bran Loaf

MAKES 1 LOAF

PREHEAT OVEN TO 350° F (180° C)
9- BY 5-INCH (2 L) LOAF PAN, LIGHTLY GREASED

This gorgeous, golden loaf becomes moister if you let it stand overnight. The challenge is to keep it from being eaten before then!

TIP

Look for a bran cereal that contains at least 10 g fiber per 1/2-cup (125 mL) serving.

Be sure you don't drain the pineapple; just spoon juice and pulp into your measuring cup.

VARIATION

Substitute brown sugar or molasses for the honey.

1 1/2 cups	all-purpose flour	375 mL
1 1/4 cups	bran cereal	300 mL
1/4 cup	granulated sugar	50 mL
2 tsp	baking soda	10 mL
1/4 tsp	salt	2 mL
2 tbsp	vegetable oil	25 mL
2	eggs	2
1/3 cup	honey	75 mL
1 1/4 cups	crushed pineapple, with juice (see Tip, at left)	300 mL

1. In a large bowl, stir together flour, bran cereal, sugar, baking soda and salt.

2. In a separate bowl, using an electric mixer, beat oil and eggs until combined. Add honey while mixing. Stir in pineapple. Pour mixture over dry ingredients and stir just until combined. Spoon into prepared pan.

3. Bake in preheated oven for 70 to 80 minutes or until a cake tester inserted in the center comes out clean. Let cool in pan on rack for 10 minutes. Remove from pan and let cool completely on rack.

Poppy Seed Oat Bread

MAKES 1 LOAF

Serve this quick bread at breakfast to enjoy the hearty goodness of oatmeal and the satisfying crunch of poppy seeds.

TIP

We prefer to use small- or medium-flake, regular or quick-cooking oats for this recipe.

VARIATION

Substitute sesame or flaxseeds for the poppy seeds. Increase the amount to 1/2 cup (125 mL).

PREHEAT OVEN TO 350° F (180° C)
9- BY 5-INCH (2 L) LOAF PAN, LIGHTLY GREASED

1 cup	whole wheat flour	250 mL
1 cup	all-purpose flour	250 mL
1 cup	quick-cooking oats	250 mL
1 tsp	baking powder	5 mL
1 tsp	baking soda	5 mL
1/2 tsp	salt	2 mL
1/4 cup	poppy seeds	50 mL
1	egg	1
1 3/4 cups	buttermilk	425 mL
1/3 cup	honey	75 mL

1. In a large bowl, stir together whole wheat flour, flour, oats, baking powder, baking soda, salt and poppy seeds.

2. In a separate bowl, using an electric mixer, beat egg and buttermilk until combined. Add honey while mixing. Pour mixture over dry ingredients and stir just until combined. Spoon into prepared pan.

3. Bake in preheated oven for 70 to 80 minutes or until a cake tester inserted in the center comes out clean. Let cool in pan on rack for 10 minutes. Remove from pan and let cool completely on rack.

Raisin Bran Bread

MAKES 1 LOAF

PREHEAT OVEN TO 350° F (180° C)
9- BY 5-INCH (2 L) LOAF PAN, LIGHTLY GREASED

Dark, heavy and sweet with molasses, this multigrain loaf is unbelievably easy to make.

1/2 cup	whole wheat flour	125 mL
2/3 cup	all-purpose flour	150 mL
2/3 cup	rye flour	150 mL
2/3 cup	bran cereal	150 mL
2/3 cup	cornmeal	150 mL
2 tsp	baking powder	10 mL
1 1/2 tsp	baking soda	7 mL
1 1/2 tsp	salt	7 mL
1 cup	raisins	250 mL
1 1/2 cups	buttermilk	375 mL
1/2 cup	molasses	125 mL

TIP

Look for a bran cereal that contains at least 10 g fiber per 1/2-cup (125 mL) serving.

VARIATION

Substitute chopped fruit – such as dates, dried apricots or dried figs – for the raisins.

1. In a large bowl, stir together whole wheat flour, flour, rye flour, bran cereal, cornmeal, baking powder, baking soda and salt. Stir in raisins.

2. In a separate bowl, using an electric mixer, beat buttermilk and molasses until combined. Pour mixture over dry ingredients and stir just until combined. Spoon into prepared pan.

3. Bake in preheated oven for 70 to 80 minutes or until a cake tester inserted in the center comes out clean. Let cool in pan on rack for 10 minutes. Remove from pan and let cool completely on rack.

Sesame Semolina Bread

MAKES 1 LOAF

PREHEAT OVEN TO 350° F (180° C)
9- BY 5-INCH (2 L) LOAF PAN, LIGHTLY GREASED

Similar to cornbread, but finer-textured, this "plain Jane" quick bread is easily dressed up with ground cardamom or ginger – or your any other spice you prefer.

1 1/4 cups	all-purpose flour	300 mL
3/4 cup	semolina flour	175 mL
2 tsp	baking powder	10 mL
1/2 tsp	salt	2 mL
1/3 cup	toasted sesame seeds (see Tip, at left)	75 mL
1/4 cup	vegetable oil	50 mL
2	eggs	2
1 1/4 cups	sour cream	300 mL
1/4 cup	honey	50 mL

TIP

For instructions on toasting sesame seeds, see Techniques Glossary, page 184.

VARIATION

For a spicy version, add 1 to 1 1/2 tsp (5 to 7 mL) ground cardamom or ginger.

Substitute pasta flour or a very fine grind of white cornmeal for the semolina.

To reduce the calories, replace the sour cream with puréed low-fat cottage cheese.

1. In a large bowl, stir together flour, semolina flour, baking powder, salt and sesame seeds. Set aside.

2. In a separate bowl, using an electric mixer, beat oil, eggs and sour cream until combined. Add honey while mixing. Pour mixture over dry ingredients and stir just until combined. Spoon into prepared pan.

3. Bake in preheated oven for 55 to 65 minutes or until a cake tester inserted in the center comes out clean. Let cool in pan on rack for 10 minutes. Remove from pan and let cool completely on rack.

Spiced Pumpkin Seed Bread

MAKES 1 LOAF

PREHEAT OVEN TO 350° F (180° C)
9- BY 5-INCH (2 L) LOAF PAN, LIGHTLY GREASED

Imagine a pumpkin pie
without the crust...

TIP

Be sure to buy pumpkin purée – not pumpkin pie filling, which is too sweet and contains too much moisture for this recipe.

VARIATION

Replace half the brown sugar with 1/3 cup (75 mL) maple syrup; combine with liquid ingredients in Step 2.

1 1/2 cups	all-purpose flour	375 mL
2/3 cup	packed brown sugar	150 mL
1 tsp	baking powder	5 mL
1 tsp	baking soda	5 mL
1/2 tsp	salt	2 mL
1 tsp	ground ginger	5 mL
1/2 tsp	ground nutmeg	2 mL
1/4 tsp	ground cloves	1 mL
1/3 cup	pumpkin seeds	75 mL
1/3 cup	sunflower seeds	75 mL
1/3 cup	vegetable oil	75 mL
2	eggs	2
1 cup	canned pumpkin purée (not pie filling)	250 mL

1. In a large bowl, stir together flour, brown sugar, baking powder, baking soda, salt, ginger, nutmeg and cloves. Stir in pumpkin seeds and sunflower seeds.

2. In a separate bowl, using an electric mixer, beat oil, eggs and pumpkin purée until combined. Pour mixture over dry ingredients and stir just until combined. Spoon into prepared pan.

3. Bake in preheated oven for 70 to 80 minutes or until a cake tester inserted in the center comes out clean. Let cool in pan on rack for 10 minutes. Remove from pan and let cool completely on rack.

Sunny Sunflower Bread

MAKES 1 LOAF

PREHEAT OVEN TO 350° F (180° C)
9- BY 5-INCH (2 L) LOAF PAN, LIGHTLY GREASED

Here the mellow sweetness of soaked apricots is complemented perfectly by the crunch of sunflower seeds and almonds. This quick bread is ideal to serve with a salad for lunch.

1 1/2 cups	boiling water	375 mL
1 cup	slivered dried apricots	250 mL
2 cups	all-purpose flour	500 mL
3/4 cup	granulated sugar	175 mL
1 tbsp	baking powder	15 mL
1/2 tsp	salt	2 mL
3/4 cup	slivered almonds	175 mL
3/4 cup	mini sunflower seeds (see Tip, at left)	175 mL
1/4 cup	vegetable oil	50 mL
1	egg	1
1 tsp	vanilla extract	5 mL

TIP

Mini sunflower seeds make the bread easier to slice. If they are not available, use the regular size.

Use raw (unroasted) unsalted sunflower seeds. For a nuttier flavor, toast seeds before using. (See Techniques Glossary, page 184, for more information.)

VARIATION

Substitute chopped hazelnuts or cashews for the almonds.

1. In a bowl pour boiling water over apricots; set aside to cool to room temperature.

2. In a large bowl, stir together flour, sugar, baking powder and salt. Stir in almonds and sunflower seeds.

3. In a separate bowl, using an electric mixer, beat oil, egg and vanilla extract until combined. Pour mixture over dry ingredients, along with apricots and soaking liquid; stir just until combined. Spoon into prepared pan.

4. Bake in preheated oven for 70 to 80 minutes or until a cake tester inserted in the center comes out clean. Let cool in pan on rack for 10 minutes. Remove from pan and let cool completely on rack.

Toasted Wheat Germ Bread

MAKES 1 LOAF

Toasting the sunflower seeds and wheat germ gives this nutritious bread a wonderfully nutty flavor.

TIP

For instructions on toasting both sunflower seeds and wheat germ, see Techniques Glossary, page 184.

Keep wheat germ in the refrigerator to prevent it from becoming rancid.

VARIATION

Substitute oat bran for the wheat bran.

For a little more tang, use plain yogurt instead of buttermilk.

3/4 cup	whole wheat flour	175 mL
1 1/2 cups	all-purpose flour	375 mL
2 tbsp	wheat bran	25 mL
1 tbsp	baking powder	15 mL
3/4 tsp	salt	4 mL
1/2 cup	toasted sunflower seeds	125 mL
2 tbsp	toasted wheat germ	25 mL
1/4 cup	vegetable oil	50 mL
2	eggs	2
1 1/4 cups	buttermilk	300 mL
1/3 cup	corn syrup	75 mL

1. In a large bowl, stir together whole wheat flour, flour, wheat bran, baking powder and salt. Stir in sunflower seeds and wheat germ.

2. In a separate bowl, using an electric mixer, beat oil, eggs and buttermilk until combined. Add corn syrup while mixing. Pour mixture over dry ingredients and stir just until combined. Spoon into prepared pan.

3. Bake in preheated oven for 70 to 80 minutes or until a cake tester inserted in the center comes out clean. Let cool in pan on rack for 10 minutes. Remove from pan and let cool completely on rack.

Wild Rice and Cranberry Loaf

MAKES 1 LOAF

See Techniques Glossary,
page 185, for instructions
on cooking wild rice.

PREHEAT OVEN TO 350° F (180° C)
9- BY 5-INCH (2 L) LOAF PAN, LIGHTLY GREASED

*The combination of wild
rice and cranberries gives
this loaf an interesting
color and texture. It's sure
to earn you compliments!*

TIP

VARIATION

Substitute unsalted
sunflower seeds or peanuts
for the pine nuts.

While the texture will
not be the same, you can
replace wild rice with
cooked long-grain white
or brown rice.

2 cups	all-purpose flour	500 mL
2 tsp	baking powder	10 mL
3/4 tsp	salt	4 mL
1 tsp	celery seeds	5 mL
1/4 tsp	black pepper	1 mL
1 cup	dried cranberries	250 mL
1 cup	cooked wild rice	250 mL
1/4 cup	pine nuts	50 mL
2 tbsp	olive oil	25 mL
2	eggs	2
1 cup	milk	250 mL
1/4 cup	honey	50 mL

1. In a large bowl, stir together flour, baking powder, salt, celery seeds and pepper. Stir in cranberries, wild rice and pine nuts.

2. In a separate bowl, using an electric mixer, beat oil, eggs and milk until combined. Add honey while mixing. Pour mixture over dry ingredients and stir just until combined. Spoon into prepared pan.

3. Bake in preheated oven for 70 to 80 minutes or until a cake tester inserted in the center comes out clean. Let cool in pan on rack for 10 minutes. Remove from pan and let cool completely on rack.

Tea Biscuits and Scones

Nothing could be faster –
or more delicious – than
freshly baked biscuits served
hot from the oven. They'll
turn any take-out entrée
into a homemade dinner!

Tips and Techniques for Tender Biscuits and Scones

The key to tender biscuits is in the gentle handling of the dough at all steps.

Cut in the butter or shortening with a pasty blender just until it resembles a coarse meal or the pieces are the size of small peas.

Mix the liquids into the dry ingredients with a fork, just until combined. Again, we don't want to overwork the dough.

Knead the dough, with a gentle hand, no more than 10 to 15 times. Remember, this isn't a yeast bread, so you don't want to develop the gluten. The dough should be soft and slightly sticky.

Roll out the dough to half the thickness you want the final biscuit. Handle the rolling pin in smooth, quick motions, rolling up at the edges to ensure the dough is the same thickness all the way to the edge.

Don't try to guess the height of the biscuit dough – use a metal or plastic ruler. Dough rolled too thinly (under 1/2 inch [1 cm]) results in heavy, tough biscuits.

For even, straight-sided biscuits, cut straight down with a floured biscuit cutter. Gently transfer the dough from the cutter directly to the baking sheet.

To get as many biscuits as possible from your first rolling of the dough, cut them out as close together as possible. These biscuits will be the most tender. Biscuits cut out from scraps rolled out a second time will be tougher and less flaky. Do not re-roll more than once.

In a hurry? Roll the dough out into a large square then cut it into smaller squares, diamonds or rectangles. There is no waste and no re-rolling needed.

For soft-sided biscuits, place them on the baking sheet so they are almost touching. For crisper sides, leave a bit more room between the biscuits.

Biscuits are done when they are golden in color, top and bottom. Remove from baking sheets as soon as possible or the bottom may become soggy.

Tips for Biscuit Toppings

Biscuit toppings can be added to fruits, vegetables, stew or chili. These dishes must be bubbling and piping hot before the topping is dropped on. The bottom of the biscuit cooks from the heat of the bubbling liquid. If the base is cold, the center and bottom of the biscuit may be gummy when the top is golden and cooked.

Drop the biscuit from one large spoon, pushing it off in one quick motion with the back of another spoon or rubber spatula. Avoid adding under-sized dollops that can cook too quickly and/or burn.

Leave a bit of room between the biscuits, allowing the liquid to bubble up. This prevents them from forming a seal that may burst and cause a sudden bubbling over into the oven.

Serve the finished dish with the biscuit placed on top of the fruit or stew. It looks more attractive this way.

Cheddar Dill Biscuits

**MAKES TWELVE
2 1/2-INCH (6 CM)
BISCUITS**

PREHEAT OVEN TO 425° F (220° C)
BAKING SHEET, UNGREASED

3/4 cup	whole wheat flour	175 mL
1 cup	all-purpose flour	250 mL
1/4 cup	rye flour	50 mL
1/4 cup	granulated sugar	50 mL
1 tbsp	baking powder	15 mL
1 tsp	baking soda	5 mL
1/4 tsp	salt	1 mL
1/4 cup	grated Parmesan cheese	50 mL
1/4 cup	snipped fresh parsley	50 mL
1 tbsp	snipped fresh dill	15 mL
1/4 cup	shortening	50 mL
1/2 cup	grated old Cheddar cheese	125 mL
1/2 cup	cottage cheese	125 mL
1/2 cup	plain yogurt	125 mL

Don't be put off by the long list of ingredients – once you taste these biscuits, you'll want to make them every week. They also freeze well. Just heat from frozen (no need to thaw) in the oven or microwave.

TIP

Vary the amount of dill according to your taste for this herb.

VARIATION

Turn these biscuits into a pizza: Make one large round, score into wedges with a pizza cutter, sprinkle extra cheese on top and bake. (Use either Parmesan or Cheddar, or both.) What a treat!

Substitute any grainy mustard for the dill.

1. In a large bowl, stir together whole wheat flour, flour, rye flour, sugar, baking powder, baking soda, salt, Parmesan cheese, parsley and dill. Using a pastry blender, cut in shortening until mixture resembles coarse crumbs. Stir in Cheddar cheese.

2. In a small bowl, combine cottage cheese and yogurt. Add all at once to dry ingredients, stirring with a fork to make a soft, but slightly sticky dough.

3. With lightly floured hands, form dough into a ball. On a lightly floured surface, knead the dough gently for 8 to 10 times. Pat or roll out the dough into a 3/4-inch (2 cm) thick round.

4. Using a 2 1/2-inch (6 cm) floured biscuit cutter, cut out as many rounds as possible. Place on baking sheet. Gently form scraps into a ball, flatten and cut out rounds.

5. Bake in preheated oven for 12 to 15 minutes. Remove from baking sheet onto a cooling rack immediately.

Currant Tea Biscuits

MAKES TWELVE 2-INCH (5 CM) BISCUITS

PREHEAT OVEN TO 425° F (220° C)
BAKING SHEET, UNGREASED

Dried currants are a traditional ingredient in tea biscuits. And here they're combined with a light, flaky texture and a hint of orange. The honey butter makes a great accompaniment to these (or any other) biscuits.

1/2 cup	dried currants	125 mL
1 cup	boiling water	250 mL
2 2/3 cups	all-purpose flour	650 mL
1/4 cup	granulated sugar	50 mL
2 tbsp	baking powder	25 mL
1/4 tsp	salt	1 mL
1 tbsp	grated orange zest	15 mL
1/3 cup	cold butter	75 mL
1 cup	milk	250 mL

HONEY BUTTER

1/2 cup	soft butter	125 mL
1/4 cup	creamed honey	50 mL
2 tsp	grated orange zest	10 mL

TIP

Be sure to dry drained currants on paper towels in Step 1. This will help to avoid heavy biscuits.

VARIATION

For a change, try using golden raisins instead of currants. Add raisins with the dry ingredients. They do not require soaking, so you can skip Step 1.

1. In a bowl pour boiling water over currants. Let stand 5 minutes. Drain currants well and pat dry on paper towels. Set aside.

2. In a large bowl, stir together flour, sugar, baking powder, salt and zest. Using a pastry blender, cut in butter until mixture resembles coarse crumbs. Stir reserved currants into dry ingredients. Add milk all at once, stirring with a fork to make a soft, but slightly sticky dough.

3. With lightly floured hands, form dough into a ball. On a lightly floured surface, knead the dough gently for 8 to 10 times. Pat or roll out the dough into a 3/4-inch (4 cm) thick round. Using a 2-inch (5 cm) floured biscuit cutter, cut out as many rounds as possible. Place on baking sheet. Gently form scraps into a ball, flatten and cut out rounds.

4. Bake in preheated oven for 12 to 15 minutes. Remove from baking sheet onto a cooling rack immediately.

5. Honey Butter: In a small bowl, cream together butter, honey and orange zest. Store, covered, in the refrigerator; bring to room temperature before serving.

Figgy Scones with Bran

MAKES 6 WEDGES

Not too many, not too few – make these to serve hot from the oven when a friend comes to visit you!

TIP

Look for a bran cereal that contains at least 10 g fiber per 1/2-cup (125 mL) serving.

You will need about 3 or 4 figs, chopped, to produce the 1/3 cup (75 mL) called for in this recipe.

VARIATION

Try using dates or raisins instead of figs.

For a different look, pat or roll out the dough into a 6-inch (15 cm) square; cut into nine 2-inch (5 cm) squares, then cut each square in half to make triangles. Bake as directed.

1/4 cup	whole wheat flour	50 mL
3/4 cup	all-purpose flour	175 mL
1 tbsp	packed brown sugar	15 mL
2 tsp	baking powder	10 mL
1/4 tsp	salt	1 mL
1/4 cup	shortening	50 mL
3/4 cup	bran cereal	175 mL
1/3 cup	chopped dried figs	75 mL
1	egg	1
1/4 cup	milk	50 mL

1. In a large bowl, stir together whole wheat flour, flour, brown sugar, baking powder and salt. Using a pastry blender, cut in shortening until mixture resembles coarse crumbs. Stir in bran cereal and figs.

2. In a small bowl, whisk together egg and milk. Add to flour mixture, stirring with a fork to make a soft, but slightly sticky dough.

3. With lightly floured hands, form dough into a ball. On a lightly floured surface, knead the dough gently for 8 to 10 times. Pat or roll out the dough into a 7-inch (17.5 cm) round. Place on prepared baking sheet. Score into 6 wedges.

4. Bake in prepared oven for 12 to 18 minutes. Remove from baking sheet onto a cooling rack immediately. Serve hot.

Fresh Tomato Basil Drop Biscuits

MAKES 18 BISCUITS

PREHEAT OVEN TO 425° F (220° C)

BAKING SHEET, LIGHTLY GREASED

Here's one of summer's best flavor combinations – the juicy sweetness of tomato and the pungent fragrance of fresh basil.

TIP

In season, use garden-fresh beefsteak tomatoes. Use an Italian plum or Roma tomato at other times of the year.

VARIATION

Substitute an equal amount of plain yogurt for the sour cream.

2 1/2 cups	all-purpose flour	625 mL
1/4 cup	granulated sugar	50 mL
2 tbsp	baking powder	25 mL
1/4 tsp	salt	1 mL
1/3 cup	snipped fresh basil	75 mL
1/3 cup	snipped fresh chives	75 mL
1/3 cup	snipped fresh parsley	75 mL
1/3 cup	shortening	75 mL
1 1/2 cups	chopped fresh tomatoes (see Tip, at left)	375 mL
1/2 cup	sour cream	125 mL

1. In a large bowl, stir together flour, sugar, baking powder, salt, basil, chives and parsley. Using a pastry blender, cut in shortening until mixture resembles coarse crumbs. Gently fold in tomatoes.

2. Add sour cream all at once, stirring with a fork to make a soft, sticky dough. Drop by heaping tablespoonfuls onto prepared pan.

3. Bake in preheated oven for 15 to 20 minutes. Remove from baking sheet onto a cooling rack immediately. Serve warm.

Rosemary Scones Topped with Caramelized Vidalias

MAKES 12 WEDGES

PREHEAT OVEN TO 425° F (220° C)
BAKING SHEET, LIGHTLY GREASED

*What a lunch treat!
Just cut into wedges and
serve hot from the oven
with a crisp salad.*

CARAMELIZED ONION TOPPING

2 tbsp	butter	25 mL
3 cups	sliced Vidalia onions	750 mL
1 tbsp	packed brown sugar	15 mL
1 tbsp	fresh rosemary leaves	15 mL
3/4 tsp	snipped fresh thyme	4 mL

TIP

For long, thin onion slices,
cut the onion in half
lengthwise before slicing.

For general instructions on
caramelizing onions to
use in other recipes,
see Techniques Glossary,
page 184.

Score the rounds with a
pizza cutter. This makes
them easy to separate
when serving.

SCONE BASE

3 cups	all-purpose flour	750 mL
1 tbsp	granulated sugar	15 mL
1 tbsp	baking powder	15 mL
1/2 tsp	baking soda	2 mL
3/4 tsp	salt	4 mL
2	cloves garlic, minced	2
3 tbsp	fresh rosemary leaves	45 mL
1/3 cup	cold butter	75 mL
1	egg	1
1 cup	buttermilk	250 mL

VARIATION

Substitute fresh oregano or
basil for the rosemary.

When Vidalias are out of
season, try using Spanish
onions instead.

1. **Topping:** In a large frying pan, melt butter over medium heat. Add onions and caramelize until tender and golden brown. Remove from heat. Add brown sugar, rosemary and thyme; set aside to cool.

2. **Scones:** In a large bowl, stir together flour, sugar, baking powder, baking soda, salt, garlic and rosemary. Using a pastry blender, cut in butter until mixture resembles coarse crumbs.

3. In a small bowl, whisk together egg and buttermilk. Add to flour mixture all at once, stirring with a fork to make a soft, slightly sticky dough.

4. With lightly floured hands, form dough into a ball. On a lightly floured surface, knead the dough gently for 8 to 10 times. Pat or roll out the dough into two 8-inch (20 cm) rounds. Place on prepared baking sheets. Score into 6 wedges each. Top with caramelized Vidalia onions.

5. Bake in prepared oven for 18 to 22 minutes. Remove from baking sheet onto a cooling rack immediately. Serve hot.

Vegetable Cobbler

SERVES 6 TO 8

PREHEAT OVEN TO 350° F (180° C)
DEEP 3-QUART (3 L) CASSEROLE DISH

This drop-biscuit-topped vegetable casserole is inspired by a recipe that originates from Romania. Although not a cobbler in the traditional sense, it's every bit as comforting.

TIP

To help to preserve the vegetables' bright color, don't lift the lid while they are cooking.

Be sure not to overcook the vegetables in Step 2. They will continue to cook as the biscuits bake.

VARIATION

Choose other vegetables you like – parsnips, turnip, potatoes, cauliflower, broccoli, eggplant and cabbage. Soft vegetables should be left in larger sizes so they cook in the same time as the harder vegetables.

Substitute your favorite fresh or dried herbs for the tarragon.

The drop biscuit in this recipe is also good on top of a chili or stew.

VEGETABLE BASE

2 cups	winter squash, cut into 1-inch (2.5 cm) cubes	500 mL
1 1/4 cups	fresh green beans, cut into 1 1/2-inch (4 cm) pieces	300 mL
2	medium carrots, cut into 1/2-inch (1 cm) slices	2
2	stalks celery, cut into 3/4-inch (2 cm) slices	2
Half	red bell pepper, cut into 3/4-inch (2 cm) strips	Half
1	medium summer squash, cut into 1-inch (2.5 cm) slices	1
2	medium tomatoes, cored and quartered	2
3	cloves garlic	3
1	bay leaf, broken in half	1
1/2 cup	chicken, beef or vegetable broth	125 mL
1/2 cup	water	125 mL
2 tbsp	olive oil	25 mL
1 tsp	salt	5 mL
1 tsp	dried tarragon leaves	5 mL

DROP BISCUIT

1/2 cup	whole wheat flour	125 mL
1/2 cup	all-purpose flour	125 mL
1/4 cup	7-grain cereal	50 mL
1 tbsp	granulated sugar	15 mL
1 1/2 tsp	baking powder	7 mL

1/2 tsp	baking soda	2 mL
1/4 tsp	salt	1 mL
3 tbsp	shortening	45 mL
2/3 cup	buttermilk	150 mL

1. **Vegetable Base:** In casserole dish, mix together squash, beans, carrots, celery, pepper, summer squash, tomatoes, garlic and bay leaf. Set aside.

2. In a small bowl, combine broth, water, olive oil, salt and tarragon. Microwave on High for 2 to 4 minutes or until hot and bubbly. Pour broth mixture over vegetables. Cover and place in the preheated oven for 35 to 45 minutes or until vegetables are tender crisp. Meanwhile, prepare the Drop Biscuit.

3. **Drop Biscuit:** In a large bowl, stir together whole wheat flour, flour, 7-grain cereal, sugar, baking powder, baking soda and salt. Using a pastry blender, cut in shortening until mixture resembles coarse crumbs. Add buttermilk all at once, stirring with a fork to make a very sticky dough. Remove vegetables from oven; leave covered. Increase oven temperature to 425° F (220° C).

4. Drop biscuit topping, by heaping tablespoonsful, onto hot bubbly vegetable mixture. Bake in preheated oven for 15 to 20 minutes. Serve immediately.

Three-Fruit Cobbler

SERVES 6 TO 8

PREHEAT OVEN TO 400° F (200° C)
DEEP 2-QUART (2 L) CASSEROLE DISH

This cobbler is a variation of the famous Nova Scotian dessert, Blueberry Grunt. It brings together some of our favorite summertime fruits – plums, peaches and pears. No spices have been added, so the natural flavors come through.

FRUIT BASE

1/3 cup	granulated sugar	75 mL
1 tbsp	cornstarch	15 mL
2 cups	coarsely chopped peaches	500 mL
2 cups	coarsely chopped pears	500 mL
2 cups	coarsely chopped plums	500 mL
1 tbsp	lemon juice	15 mL

COBBLER DROP BISCUIT

1 cup	all-purpose flour	250 mL
1/4 cup	granulated sugar	50 mL
1/2 tsp	baking powder	2 mL
1/2 tsp	baking soda	2 mL
1/4 tsp	salt	1 mL
1/4 cup	cold butter	50 mL
1/2 cup	buttermilk	125 mL

TIP

No need to peel the tender fruits; the skins will soften as the cobbler bakes.

Cut fruit into quarters or eighths, depending on size.

For best results, fruit should be perfectly ripe. If necessary, ripen fruit in a paper bag on the counter until fragrant and yields to gentle pressure.

Three medium peaches, pears or nectarines yield 2 cups (500 mL) coarsely chopped; 4 plums yield 2 cups (500 mL) chopped.

See "Tips and Techniques for Tender Biscuits and Scones," page 54.

VARIATION

Use apples, raspberries and pears (or another combination of seasonal fruit) to make up 6 cups (1.5 L) in total.

1. **Fruit Base:** In casserole dish, mix together sugar and cornstarch. Stir in peaches, pears, plums and lemon juice. Microwave on High for 6 to 8 minutes or until hot and bubbly, stirring once. (Or place in preheated oven until heated through.)

2. **Drop Biscuit:** In a large bowl, stir together flour, sugar, baking powder, baking soda and salt. Using a pastry blender; cut in butter until mixture resembles coarse crumbs. Add buttermilk all at once, stirring with a fork to make a very sticky dough. Drop by heaping tablespoonfuls onto hot bubbly fruit mixture.

3. Bake in preheated oven for 20 to 25 minutes. Serve warm.

CHERRY STREUSEL COFFEE CAKE (PAGE 72) ➤

White Chocolate Macadamia Drop Biscuits

MAKES SEVEN 2-INCH (5 CM) BISCUITS

PREHEAT OVEN TO 425° F (220° C)

BAKING SHEET, LIGHTLY GREASED

Here's the ultimate in decadent enjoyment. So forget about the guilt – just go ahead and enjoy!

1 1/2 cups	all-purpose flour	375 mL
1/4 cup	granulated sugar	50 mL
1 tbsp	baking powder	15 mL
1/8 tsp	salt	0.5 mL
1/4 cup	butter	50 mL
2/3 cup	macadamia nuts	150 mL
2/3 cup	white chocolate chips	150 mL
1/2 cup	milk	125 mL

TIP

Scoop the batter onto a large serving spoon and push it off onto the baking sheet with the back of another. The less you handle the batter, the lighter the biscuits.

VARIATION

We could suggest alternative ingredients, but why bother? You can't improve upon the combination of white chocolate and macadamia nuts!

1. In a large bowl, stir together flour, sugar, baking powder and salt. Using a pastry blender, cut in butter until mixture resembles coarse crumbs.

2. Stir in macadamia nuts and chips. Add milk all at once, stirring with a fork to make a soft, sticky dough. Drop by heaping tablespoonfuls onto prepared pan.

3. Bake in preheated oven for 12 to 15 minutes. Remove from baking sheet onto a cooling rack immediately. Serve warm.

◄ CHOCOLATE ORANGE WAFFLES (PAGE 89)

Whole Wheat Poppy Biscuits

**MAKES EIGHTEEN
2-INCH (5 CM) BISCUITS**

If you love poppy seeds, these biscuits are heaven-sent.

TIP

Adjust the quantity of poppy seeds to your taste.

For browner, crisper tops, bake biscuits in the upper third of the oven.

VARIATION

Poppy seeds can be replaced with any other small seed – such as sesame, caraway, fennel, anise or mini sunflower seeds. For stronger-flavored seeds, you may wish to reduce the quantity used.

PREHEAT OVEN TO 425° F (220° C)
BAKING SHEET, LIGHTLY GREASED

1 1/2 cups	whole wheat flour	375 mL
1 cup	all-purpose flour	250 mL
1/4 cup	granulated sugar	50 mL
1/4 cup	poppy seeds	50 mL
1 tbsp	baking powder	15 mL
1/2 tsp	baking soda	2 mL
1/2 tsp	salt	2 mL
1/3 cup	shortening	75 mL
1 cup	buttermilk	250 mL

1. In a large bowl, stir together whole wheat flour, flour, sugar, poppy seeds, baking powder, baking soda and salt. Using a pastry blender, cut in shortening until mixture resembles coarse crumbs. Add buttermilk all at once, stirring with a fork to make a soft, but slightly sticky dough.

2. With lightly floured hands, form dough into a ball. On a lightly floured surface, knead the dough gently for 8 to 10 times. Pat or roll out the dough into a 1/2-inch (1 cm) thick round.

3. Using a 2-inch (5 cm) floured biscuit cutter, cut out as many rounds as possible. Place on baking sheet. Gently form scraps into a ball, flatten and cut out rounds.

4. Bake in preheated oven for 12 to 15 minutes. Remove from baking sheet onto a cooling rack immediately. Serve warm.

Brunch Cakes, Coffee Cakes and Snacking Cakes

E qually good as a special luncheon dessert or a mid-afternoon treat, these cakes include some of our favorite flavor combinations. Served warm from the oven, they are always welcome.

Tips for Storing, Icing and Serving Coffee Cakes

Once you remove the cake from the oven, follow the cooling directions in the recipe. In general, most coffee cakes should be cooled on a wire rack for 10 minutes before removing from the pan. If you wait too long, and the cake sticks to the pan, return it to the oven for 1 to 2 minutes, then try to remove it.

You may need to run a rubber spatula around the edge of the cake in order to loosen it from the sides of the pan. Be careful not to cut the cake or scratch the pan by using a knife or metal spatula. When baking in a springform pan, let the cake cool for 10 minutes in the pan before removing the sides, cool 30 minutes, then slide it off the base onto a flat cake plate to serve.

Do not cover or store cakes until they are completely cooled. Similarly, they should be cooled before filling, frosting or glazing unless the recipe directs otherwise.

To avoid crumbling, it is generally considered best to allow cakes to cool to room temperature before slicing. However, we have found that coffee cakes and quick breads can be sliced successfully with an electric knife, even when hot from the oven.

Coffee cakes freeze well. Cool completely before wrapping airtight for the freezer. Slice or pre-portion into family-sized pieces before wrapping. Always over-wrap coffee cakes before freezing. Label and date cakes, then freeze for up to 6 weeks. Thaw in the refrigerator, while still wrapped, to prevent drying.

For short-term storage, cakes can be tightly wrapped and kept at room temperature for 2 to 3 days. (In fact, coffee cakes often become stale more quickly if kept in the refrigerator.) When storing at room temperature, watch for the development of mold – particularly during hot, humid weather.

For a perfect after-school treat, wrap individual portions of quick bread in airtight plastic wrap or in a sandwich bag, then place in a freezer bag and freeze. To serve immediately, thaw on a plate, unwrapped, in the microwave for 30 seconds on High. Or place frozen in lunch bags in the morning; it will be ready to enjoy by noon.

For a fresher, more attractive appearance, thaw the cake, glaze, then decorate with toasted nuts and fruit wedges.

Banana Chocolate Chip Coffee Cake

MAKES 1 CAKE

PREHEAT OVEN TO 350° F (180° C)
9-INCH SQUARE (2.5 L) PAN, LIGHTLY GREASED

*What a combination –
bananas, coffee and
chocolate! These are three
of our favorite things.*

TIP

Mash and freeze ripe
bananas so they're ready
when you need them. Thaw
and warm to room
temperature before using.

For a quick and easy glaze,
set aside half the mini chips
called for in the recipe and
sprinkle on top of batter
before baking.

VARIATION

If you prefer a chocolate-
banana rather than mocha-
banana flavor, omit the
coffee granules.

For a slightly higher cake,
use an 8-inch (2 L) square
pan. It may take a few
extra minutes to bake.

2 cups	all-purpose flour	500 mL
1 tsp	baking powder	5 mL
1/2 tsp	baking soda	2 mL
1/2 tsp	salt	2 mL
1 tbsp	instant coffee granules	15 mL
1 tbsp	hot water	15 mL
1 1/3 cups	mashed bananas	325 mL
1/2 cup	soft butter	125 mL
3/4 cup	granulated sugar	175 mL
1	egg	1
1 cup	mini-chocolate chips	250 mL

1. In a large bowl, stir together flour, baking powder, baking soda and salt; set aside.

2. In a small bowl, dissolve coffee granules in water. Add bananas; set aside.

3. In a separate large bowl, using an electric mixer, cream butter, sugar and egg until light and fluffy. Stir in dry ingredients alternately with banana mixture, making 3 additions of dry ingredients and 2 of banana; stir just until combined after each addition. Stir in the chocolate chips. Spoon into prepared pan.

4. Bake in preheated oven for 55 to 65 minutes or until a cake tester inserted in the center comes out clean. Let cool in pan on rack for 10 minutes. Remove from pan and let cool completely on rack.

Apple Upside-Down Coffee Cake

MAKES 1 CAKE

Sweetened with apple-sauce and lightly spiced with cinnamon, this coffee cake provides delicious, comforting flavor in every bite. Just pop it into the oven and wait for the compliments!

TIP

To prevent the top from browning too quickly, bake on the bottom rack of the oven.

If the base does not fit tightly into the sides of your springform pan, wrap the bottom in aluminum foil or place the pan on a baking sheet during baking.

VARIATION

For a built-in garnish on the top of coffee cake, arrange the apples in overlapping circles in the bottom of the pan.

PREHEAT OVEN TO 350° F (180° C)
9-INCH (2.5 L) SPRINGFORM PAN, LIGHTLY GREASED

APPLE BASE

1/3 cup	packed brown sugar	75 mL
2 tbsp	unsweetened applesauce	25 mL
1 tsp	ground cinnamon	5 mL
4 cups	sliced apples	1 L

COFFEE CAKE

2 cups	all-purpose flour	500 mL
2 tsp	baking powder	10 mL
1 tsp	baking soda	5 mL
1 tsp	ground cinnamon	5 mL
1/4 tsp	salt	1 mL
1/2 cup	plain yogurt	125 mL
1/2 cup	unsweetened applesauce	125 mL
1/3 cup	soft butter	75 mL
1/2 cup	granulated sugar	125 mL
2	eggs	2
1 tsp	vanilla extract	5 mL

1. In a small bowl, combine brown sugar, applesauce and cinnamon; spread over bottom of prepared pan. Arrange apple slices in the applesauce mixture.

2. In a large bowl, stir together flour, baking powder, baking soda, cinnamon and salt; set aside.

3. In a small bowl, combine yogurt and applesauce; set aside.

4. In a separate large bowl, using an electric mixer, cream butter, sugar, eggs and vanilla extract until light and fluffy. Stir in dry ingredients alternately with yogurt mixture, making 3 additions of dry ingredients and 2 of yogurt; stir just until combined after each addition. Spoon over apples in prepared pan.

5. Bake in preheated oven for 55 to 65 minutes or until a cake tester inserted in the center comes out clean. Immediately invert on a flat plate. Remove pan and serve warm.

Cherry Streusel Coffee Cake

MAKES 1 CAKE

PREHEAT OVEN TO 350° F (180° C)

10-INCH (3 L) SPRINGFORM PAN, LIGHTLY GREASED

A holiday brunch isn't complete without a coffee cake served fresh from the oven. During this busy season, try our quick, convenient, timesaving version. The almonds toast as the coffee cake bakes.

TIP

When you add lemon juice to the evaporated milk, it will appear to have curdled. Don't worry – this is normal.

VARIATION

Raspberry, apple or peach pie filling can be substituted for the cherry.

COFFEE CAKE

3/4 cup	evaporated milk	175 mL
1 tbsp	lemon juice	15 mL
2 1/4 cups	all-purpose flour	550 mL
3/4 cup	granulated sugar	175 mL
1/2 tsp	baking powder	2 mL
1/2 tsp	baking soda	2 mL
1/4 tsp	salt	1 mL
2/3 cup	cold butter	150 mL
1	egg	1
1 tsp	almond extract	5 mL

FRUIT FILLING

2 cups	cherry pie filling	500 mL
1/2 cup	sliced almonds	125 mL

1. In a small bowl, combine evaporated milk and lemon juice; set aside for 5 minutes.

2. In a large bowl, stir together flour, sugar, baking powder, baking soda and salt. Using a pastry blender; cut in butter until mixture resembles coarse crumbs. Remove 1/2 cup (125 mL) of the mixture; set aside for topping.

3. In a separate bowl, using an electric mixer, beat egg, almond extract and evaporated milk/lemon mixture until combined. Pour over flour mixture and stir just until combined. Spoon two-thirds into prepared pan.

4. Spread pie filling over coffee cake batter, leaving a 1-inch (2.5 cm) rim around the edge. Top with remaining third of batter. Spread carefully to cover filling. Sprinkle with reserved crumb topping and sliced almonds.

5. Bake in preheated oven for 70 to 80 minutes or until a cake tester inserted in the center comes out clean. Let cool in pan on rack for 10 minutes. Remove the sides from the pan and let cool 30 minutes. Slide from the bottom of the pan onto a flat cake plate.

Coffee Toffee Coffee Cake

MAKES 1 CAKE

PREHEAT OVEN TO 350° F (180° C)
9-INCH (2.5 L) SPRINGFORM PAN, LIGHTLY GREASED

This cake is so irresistible, Donna's daughters-in-law have been observed microwaving slices straight from the freezer to top with chocolate ice cream and fresh strawberries.

TOFFEE TOPPING

1/4 cup	packed brown sugar	50 mL
1/3 cup	all-purpose flour	75 mL
1 1/2 tsp	ground cinnamon	7 mL
1 tsp	instant coffee granules	5 mL
2 tbsp	cold butter	25 mL
3/4 cup	toffee bits	175 mL
1/2 cup	chopped pecans	125 mL

COFFEE CAKE

3 tbsp	instant coffee granules	45 mL
2 tbsp	Swiss chocolate almond liqueur	25 mL
2 cups	all-purpose flour	500 mL
1 tbsp	baking powder	15 mL
1/2 tsp	baking soda	2 mL
1/2 tsp	salt	2 mL
1/3 cup	soft butter	75 mL
3/4 cup	granulated sugar	175 mL
2	eggs	2
3/4 cup	sour cream	175 mL

TIP

Don't add more toffee bits than are called for in the recipe; if you do, the topping will become brittle, instead of crumbly and crunchy.

VARIATION

Substitute unsweetened orange juice concentrate for the liqueur.

For a mocha version of this cake, replace 1 tbsp (15 mL) of the cocoa with an equal amount of coffee granules, and substitute chocolate chips for the toffee bits in the topping.

1. **Toffee Topping:** In a large bowl, combine brown sugar, flour, cinnamon and coffee granules. With a pastry blender, cut in butter until crumbly. Add toffee bits and pecans; set aside.

2. **Coffee Cake:** In a small bowl, dissolve coffee granules in liqueur; set aside 5 minutes.

3. In a large bowl, stir together flour, baking powder, baking soda and salt; set aside.

4. In a separate large bowl, using an electric mixer, cream butter, sugar and eggs until light and fluffy. Stir in coffee mixture. Stir in dry ingredients alternately with sour cream, making 3 additions of dry ingredients and 2 of sour cream; stir just until combined after each addition. Spoon into prepared pan. Sprinkle toffee topping over coffee cake batter.

5. Bake in preheated oven for 55 to 65 minutes or until a cake tester inserted in the center comes out clean. Let cool in pan on rack for 10 minutes. Remove sides from pan and allow to cool for 30 minutes. Slide from bottom of pan onto a flat cake plate.

Cranberry Crumble Coffee Cake

MAKES 1 CAKE

PREHEAT OVEN TO 350° F (180° C)

8-INCH (2 L) PAN, LIGHTLY GREASED

Each slice is dotted with bright red cranberries and flavored with a hint of orange.

PECAN TOPPING

1/3 cup	packed brown sugar	75 mL
2 tbsp	all-purpose flour	10 mL
2 tbsp	cold butter	10 mL
3/4 cup	finely chopped pecans	175 mL

COFFEE CAKE

2 cups	all-purpose flour	500 mL
2/3 cup	granulated sugar	150 mL
1 1/2 tsp	baking powder	7 mL
1/2 tsp	salt	2 mL
2 tbsp	grated orange zest	25 mL
1/2 tsp	ground allspice	2 mL
1/2 tsp	ground nutmeg	2 mL
1/4 cup	vegetable oil	50 mL
1	egg	1
1 cup	unsweetened orange juice	250 mL
2 cups	frozen cranberries	500 mL

TIP

No need to thaw the cranberries; they'll cook while the coffee cake is baking. In fact leaving them frozen will help to prevent them from "bleeding" into the bread.

VARIATION

An equal amount of fresh cranberries can be substituted for the frozen. Add with the dry ingredients.

Substitute 1/4 cup (50 mL) thawed frozen cranberry juice concentrate and 3/4 cup (175 mL) orange juice for the 1 cup (250 mL) orange juice.

1. **Pecan Topping:** In a large bowl, combine brown sugar and flour. With a pastry blender, cut in butter until crumbly. Add pecans; set aside.

2. In a large bowl, stir together flour, sugar, baking powder, salt, zest, allspice and nutmeg; set aside.

3. In a separate bowl, using an electric mixer, beat oil, egg and orange juice until combined. Pour over flour mixture and stir just until combined. Fold in cranberries. Spoon into prepared pan. Sprinkle pecan topping over coffee cake batter.

4. Bake in preheated oven for 70 to 80 minutes or until a cake tester inserted in the center comes out clean. Let cool in pan on rack for 10 minutes. Remove from pan and let cool completely on rack.

Gingerbread with Warm Lemon Sauce

MAKES 1 GINGERBREAD

PREHEAT OVEN TO 350° F (180° C)

8-INCH (2 L) BAKING PAN, LIGHTLY GREASED

The tangy lemon sauce is what really makes this traditional gingerbread into something special. In fact, to make sure you don't run out, we suggest that you double the sauce recipe!

TIP

Even though the gingerbread batter appears thin, resist the urge to add more flour. Beat only until smooth.

VARIATION

Try the Lemon Sauce drizzled over ORANGE PUMPKIN SNACKING CAKE (see recipe, page 80).

1 cup	boiling water	250 mL
1/2 cup	shortening	125 mL
1 3/4 cups	all-purpose flour	425 mL
1/2 tsp	baking powder	2 mL
1/4 tsp	baking soda	1 mL
1/4 tsp	salt	1 mL
1 1/2 tsp	ground ginger	7 mL
3/4 tsp	ground cinnamon	4 mL
2/3 cup	granulated sugar	150 mL
2	eggs	2
2/3 cup	molasses	150 mL

LEMON SAUCE

3 tbsp	butter	45 mL
1/2 cup	granulated sugar	125 mL
3 tbsp	cornstarch	45 mL
1 1/3 cups	water	325 mL
2 tsp	grated lemon zest	10 mL
1/3 cup	lemon juice	75 mL

1. In a small bowl, pour boiling water over shortening; set aside to soften.

2. In a large bowl, stir together flour, baking powder, baking soda, salt, ginger and cinnamon; set aside.

3. In a separate large bowl, using an electric mixer, mix sugar, eggs and molasses. Add shortening mixture and beat until smooth. Stir in dry ingredients; mix just until blended. Pour into prepared pan.

4. Bake in preheated oven for 45 to 55 minutes or until a cake tester inserted in the center comes out clean. Immediately invert on a cooling rack. Remove pan and serve warm with lemon sauce.

5. Lemon Sauce: In a bowl microwave butter on High for 15 to 20 seconds or until melted. In another bowl, mix together sugar and cornstarch; add water, lemon zest, lemon juice and melted butter. Microwave on High for 3 to 5 minutes or until boiling and thickened, stirring once or twice. Makes 2 cups (500 mL).

Orange Pumpkin Snacking Cake

MAKES 1 CAKE

No time to make a pumpkin pie for Thanksgiving dinner? Try serving this snacking cake instead.

TIP

Be sure to buy pumpkin purée – not pumpkin pie filling, which is too sweet and contains too much moisture for this snacking cake.

VARIATION

Substitute 2 to 3 tsp (10 to 15 mL) pumpkin pie spice for the individual spices.

PREHEAT OVEN TO 350° F (180° C)
9-INCH (2.5 L) SPRINGFORM PAN, LIGHTLY GREASED

1 cup	whole wheat flour	250 mL
2 cups	all-purpose flour	500 mL
3/4 cup	packed brown sugar	175 mL
1 tbsp	grated orange zest	15 mL
1 tbsp	baking powder	15 mL
1 tsp	baking soda	5 mL
1 tsp	ground cinnamon	5 mL
1/2 tsp	ground allspice	2 mL
1/2 tsp	ground ginger	2 mL
1/2 tsp	ground nutmeg	2 mL
1/4 tsp	ground cloves	1 mL
1/2 cup	vegetable oil	125 mL
3	eggs	3
1 1/4 cups	canned pumpkin purée (not pie filling)	300 mL
1/2 cup	orange juice	125 mL
1 cup	chopped pecans	250 mL

1. In a large bowl, stir together whole wheat flour, flour, brown sugar, zest, baking powder, baking soda, cinnamon, allspice, ginger, nutmeg and cloves; set aside.

2. In a separate bowl, using an electric mixer, beat oil, eggs, pumpkin purée and orange juice until combined. Pour mixture over dry ingredients and stir just until combined. Stir in pecans. Spoon into prepared pan.

3. Bake in preheated oven for 60 to 70 minutes or until a cake tester inserted in the center comes out clean. Immediately invert on a cooling rack. Remove pan and let cool completely.

Peach Pinwheel Brunch Cake

MAKES 1 CAKE

Here's the ideal cake to prepare when baskets of ripe fresh peaches are plentiful at your local farmers market. The delightful moistness and texture is like a cheesecake – but without all the fat and cholesterol.

TIP

It's easy to peel peaches if you blanch them first.

Don't try to bake this cake in a springform pan, or the sauce will drip out the bottom. We speak from experience!

VARIATION

When fresh peaches are out of season, substitute well-drained, water-packed canned peaches.

Try this recipe using nectarines and/or plums instead of peaches.

PREHEAT OVEN TO 350° F (180° C)
9-INCH (2.5 L) SQUARE PAN, LIGHTLY GREASED

1 1/2 cups	all-purpose flour	375 mL
1 1/2 tsp	baking powder	7 mL
3/4 tsp	salt	7 mL
1/3 cup	shortening	75 mL
1 cup	granulated sugar	250 mL
1	egg	1
1 tsp	almond extract	5 mL
1 cup	sour cream	250 mL
2 cups	chopped peaches	500 mL
2 cups	sliced peaches (See Variation, at left)	500 mL

1. In a large bowl, stir together flour, baking powder and salt; set aside.

2. In a separate large bowl, using an electric mixer, cream shortening, sugar, egg and almond extract until light and fluffy. Stir in dry ingredients alternately with sour cream, making 3 additions of dry ingredients and 2 of sour cream; stir just until combined after each addition. Fold in chopped peaches. Spoon into prepared pan. Top with peach slices.

3. Bake in preheated oven for 55 to 65 minutes or until a cake tester inserted in the center comes out clean. Let cool in pan on a cooling rack.

Walnut Swirl Crumb Brunch Cake

MAKES 1 CAKE

PREHEAT OVEN TO 350° F (180° C)

8-INCH (2 L) SQUARE PAN, LIGHTLY GREASED

Expecting guests for brunch? You can't miss with this ever-popular coffee cake.

WALNUT CRUMB FILLING

1 cup	coarsely chopped walnuts	250 mL
1/2 cup	packed brown sugar	125 mL
2 tsp	ground cinnamon	10 mL

CAKE

1 1/2 cups	all-purpose flour	375 mL
2 tsp	baking powder	10 mL
1/2 tsp	salt	2 mL
1/3 cup	soft butter	75 mL
2/3 cup	granulated sugar	150 mL
2	eggs	2
1 tsp	vanilla	5 mL
1 1/3 cups	sour cream	325 mL

TIP

Prepare cake the day before, wrap, and keep at room temperature. It will stay moist. Warm in the oven for a few minutes before serving.

VARIATION

For a streusel effect, spoon all the batter into the pan and sprinkle the Walnut Crumb Filling on the top.

Substitute either plain or fruit-flavored yogurt for the sour cream.

1. **Walnut Crumb Filling:** In a small bowl, combine walnuts, brown sugar and cinnamon; set aside.

2. In a large bowl, stir together flour, baking powder and salt; set aside

3. In a separate large bowl, using an electric mixer, cream butter, sugar, eggs and vanilla until light and fluffy. Stir in dry ingredients alternately with sour cream, making 3 additions of dry ingredients and 2 of sour cream; stir just until combined after each addition.

4. Spoon one-half of the batter into prepared pan. Sprinkle with walnut crumb filling. Spoon remaining batter over filling. Pull a knife through the batter in wide curves. Rotate pan one-quarter turn and repeat for marble effect.

5. Bake in preheated oven for 50 to 60 minutes or until a cake tester inserted in the center comes out clean. Let cool in pan on rack for 10 minutes. Remove from pan. Serve warm.

Crêpes, Pancakes and Waffles

From hearty breakfast fare to elegant desserts, pancakes, waffles and crêpes take the simplest of ingredients and transform them into dishes worth celebrating.

Tips and Techniques for...

Perfect Pancakes

Very lightly coat the grill or griddle with vegetable oil or a cooking spray – not too much, or you'll get dark and light rings on the bottom of the pancake.

Heat just until moderately hot. Drops of cold water should dance across the surface. It is too hot when the water sizzles and evaporates quickly.

For tender pancakes, mix batter only until lumpy.

Turn pancakes only once. Wait until the edges are bubbly (and bubbles begin to break through the surface) before turning. If pancakes stick, leave a few more seconds and try again – they will often loosen themselves from the grill when it's time to turn. The first side cooks in 2 minutes and the second side takes about half that time. Cook just until golden.

Pancakes don't have to be made and eaten immediately. The batter can stand, covered, in the refrigerator overnight. There's no need to bring the batter back to room temperature; just stir to mix, then ladle onto the grill. Cooked pancakes can be reheated in a 350° F (180° C) oven for 3 to 5 minutes or popped frozen into the toaster.

Wonderful Waffles

Thin batters result in more tender waffles than thick batters.

Separate the eggs, whip the whites and fold back in for lighter waffles.

Be sure to preheat the waffle maker.

Clean the waffle maker by brushing out the crumbs with a soft brush. The factory-applied coating on the waffle maker's cooking surface is harmed by water. You may occasionally need to oil the waffle maker, but do so sparingly or the waffles will be greasy.

Classic Crêpes

A well-seasoned crêpe pan should be oiled only very lightly. Wipe out excess oil with a paper towel. Too much oil results in greasy crêpes. Additional applications of oil will be needed only occasionally or not at all.

The batter should be thin, smooth and lump-free. (Sieve out any remaining lumps.)

Add a bit of sugar to the batter for slightly sweeter dessert crêpes.

Refrigerating batter at least an hour (preferably overnight) results in more tender crêpes.

The secret of making perfect crêpes is simple: practice, practice, practice! In fact, the first crêpe of every batch is just that – a practice one! Ladle the batter into the hot pan, tilting the pan and swirling the batter just to coat the bottom evenly. This should be done quickly so the pan does not cool. If there's too much batter, the resulting crêpe will be thick and gummy.

Return pan to the heat for a minute until crêpe is a light golden brown. Turn by lifting one corner with your fingertips or with a heatproof non-metallic spatula. Be careful – it's hot!

Cook the second side for another 30 seconds or just until lightly browned then, using the pan, slide it onto a stack. The first side will have browned more than the second, so use it as the outside when rolling the crêpe.

Make crêpes ahead and store in the refrigerator for 2 to 3 days or in the freezer for several weeks. Stack between sheets of waxed or parchment paper in an airtight freezer bag. Thaw before removing from the package or they may tear.

Buttermilk Waffles

MAKES 8 LARGE WAFFLES

WAFFLE MAKER, LIGHTLY GREASED

The classic breakfast treat for lazy weekend mornings, these waffles can also be made ahead and enjoyed throughout the week.

3 cups	all-purpose flour	750 mL
1/4 cup	granulated sugar	50 mL
1 1/2 tsp	baking powder	7 mL
1/2 tsp	baking soda	2 mL
1/2 tsp	salt	2 mL
2 cups	buttermilk	500 mL
1 cup	milk	250 mL
1/4 cup	vegetable oil	50 mL
3	eggs, separated	3

TIP

To store extra waffles, separate each with a layer of waxed paper, then keep in the refrigerator for 2 or 3 days, or freeze in a heavy plastic freezer bag. Reheat in a microwave or pop frozen into the toaster.

For information about preheating waffle maker, see Techniques Glossary, page 185.

For instructions on how to whip egg whites to stiff peaks, see Techniques Glossary, page 185.

VARIATION

Try sprinkling a few frozen blueberries on the batter in the waffle maker, just before closing the top.

1. In a large bowl, stir together flour, sugar, baking powder, baking soda and salt.

2. In a small bowl, whisk together buttermilk, milk, oil and egg yolks. Add milk mixture to dry ingredients, all at once, stirring with a few quick strokes, just until combined.

3. In a separate small bowl, using an electric mixer, beat egg whites until stiff (but not dry) peaks form; fold into batter. Mixture should be lumpy.

4. Heat waffle maker until medium hot. Pour in just enough batter to fill about two-thirds full. Close lid and cook for 3 minutes or until no longer steaming. Repeat with remaining batter.

Apple Crêpes

MAKES TWELVE 6-INCH (15 CM) CRÊPES

This make-ahead dessert can be warmed and assembled at the last minute for your next dinner party.

TIP

The apple filling can be quickly prepared in the microwave.

VARIATION

Substitute your favorite prepared fruit pie filling for the apple filling.

SIX-INCH (15 CM) CRÊPE PAN OR FRYPAN, LIGHTLY GREASED

CRÊPES

2/3 cup	all-purpose flour	150 mL
2 tsp	granulated sugar	10 mL
1/2 tsp	salt	2 mL
2/3 cup	milk	150 mL
1/3 cup	water	75 mL
1 tbsp	melted butter	15 mL
2	eggs	2

APPLE FILLING

1/3 cup	butter	75 mL
1 cup	packed brown sugar	250 mL
1/2 tsp	ground cinnamon	2 mL
6 cups	sliced apples	1.5 L

1. **Crêpes:** In a large bowl, stir together flour, sugar and salt.

2. In a small bowl, whisk together milk, water, melted butter and eggs. Pour mixture over dry ingredients all at once, stirring until smooth. Cover and refrigerate for at least 1 hour or preferably overnight. Bring batter back to room temperature before using.

3. Heat pan until medium-hot. Add 3 tbsp (45 mL) batter for each crêpe, tilting and rotating pan to ensure batter covers entire bottom of pan. Cook for 1 1/2 to 2 minutes or until the edges begin to brown. Turn carefully with a non-metal spatula or fingertips. Cook for another 30 to 45 seconds. Remove to a plate and repeat with remaining batter.

4. **Filling:** Melt butter. Stir in sugar and cinnamon. Add apples and simmer gently until tender. Spread 1/4 to 1/3 cup (50 to 75 mL) hot apple filling down the center of each warm crêpe, roll and served topped with a sprinkle of cinnamon.

Asparagus- and Ham-Filled Crêpes

MAKES TWELVE 6-INCH (15 CM) CRÊPES

Invite a group of your favorite friends to lunch, and serve these savory crêpes, hot or cold, topped with corn relish. They'll be a sure hit!

TIP

The crêpes can be made ahead and frozen. Thaw before filling.

For more information about making crêpes, see page 84.

VARIATION

Substitute a fruit chutney or salsa for the corn relish.

SIX-INCH (15 CM) CRÊPE PAN OR FRYPAN, LIGHTLY GREASED

CRÊPES

2/3 cup	all-purpose flour	150 mL
2 tsp	granulated sugar	10 mL
1/4 tsp	salt	1 mL
2/3 cup	milk	150 mL
1/3 cup	water	75 mL
1 tbsp	melted butter	15 mL
2	eggs	2

ASPARAGUS HAM FILLING

12	slices Black Forest ham (about 1 oz [25 g])	12
36	stalks asparagus, steamed	36
1 1/2 cups	corn relish	375 mL

1. **Crêpes:** In a large bowl, stir together flour, sugar and salt.

2. In a small bowl, whisk together milk, water, melted butter and eggs. Pour mixture over dry ingredients all at once, whisking until smooth. Cover and refrigerate for at least 1 hour or preferably overnight. Bring batter back to room temperature before using.

3. Heat pan until medium-hot. Add 3 tbsp (45 mL) batter for each crêpe, tilting and rotating the pan to ensure the batter covers the entire bottom of the pan. Cook batter for 1 1/2 to 2 minutes or until the edges begin to brown. Turn carefully with a non-metal spatula or fingertips. Cook for another 30 to 45 seconds. Remove to a plate and repeat with remaining batter.

4. **Filling:** Place a slice of ham and 3 asparagus spears down the center of each warm crêpe, roll and place seam side down on serving plate. Warm in microwave, if desired. Top with corn relish.

Chocolate Crêpes with Fresh Strawberries

MAKES TWELVE 6-INCH (15 CM) CRÊPES

This elegant low-cal favorite makes the ideal finish to an elegant dinner party.

TIP

To prevent lumps, sieve the cocoa, then mix well with the other dry ingredients before adding the liquids.

Prepare the crêpes ahead and bring to room temperature, covered. Arrange 1 or 2 on each plate to serve.

VARIATION

Try a combination of strawberries with other fruits, such as sliced bananas, pineapple and kiwi.

SIX-INCH (15 CM) CRÊPE PAN OR FRYPAN, LIGHTLY GREASED

CRÊPES

2/3 cup	all-purpose flour	150 mL
2 tbsp	unsweetened cocoa	25 mL
2 tbsp	granulated sugar	25 mL
Pinch	salt	Pinch
2/3 cup	milk	150 mL
1/3 cup	water	75 mL
1 tbsp	melted butter	15 mL
2	eggs	2

1. **Crêpes:** In a large bowl, stir together flour, cocoa, sugar and salt.

2. In a small bowl, whisk together milk, water, melted butter and eggs. Pour mixture over dry ingredients all at once, stirring until smooth. Cover and refrigerate for at least 1 hour or preferably overnight. Bring batter back to room temperature before using.

3. Heat pan until medium hot. Add 3 tbsp (45 mL) batter for each crêpe, tilting and rotating pan to ensure batter covers entire bottom of pan. Cook for 1 1/2 to 2 minutes or until the edges begin to brown. Turn carefully with a non-metal spatula or fingertips. Cook for another 30 to 45 seconds. Remove to a plate and repeat with remaining batter.

4. **To serve:** Fold crêpes in half, then in quarters. Top with fresh fruit and drizzle with chocolate sauce.

Chocolate Orange Waffles

**MAKES 10
LARGE WAFFLES**

*Orange and chocolate are
two flavors that just naturally go together. These
waffles are irresistible to
children – adults too!*

TIP

To store extra waffles, separate each with a layer of
waxed paper, then keep in
the refrigerator for 2 or 3
days, or freeze in a heavy
plastic freezer bag. Reheat
in a microwave or pop
frozen into the toaster.

VARIATION

Top with fresh strawberries
and drizzle with chocolate
syrup. For a gourmet touch,
dust with confectioners
(icing) sugar pressed
through a sieve.

WAFFLE MAKER, LIGHTLY GREASED

1 cup	all-purpose flour	250 mL
2/3 cup	granulated sugar	150 mL
1/2 cup	unsweetened cocoa	125 mL
1/2 tsp	baking powder	2 mL
1/2 tsp	baking soda	2 mL
1/4 tsp	salt	1 mL
1 tbsp	grated orange zest	15 mL
1/4 cup	vegetable oil	50 mL
2	eggs, separated	2
1 cup	yogurt	250 mL

1. In a large bowl, stir together flour, sugar, cocoa, baking powder, baking soda, salt and zest.

2. In a small bowl, whisk together oil, egg yolks and yogurt. Pour mixture over dry ingredients all at once, stirring with a few quick strokes, just until combined.

3. In a separate small bowl, using an electric mixer, beat egg whites until stiff but not dry peaks form; fold into batter. Mixture should be lumpy.

4. Heat waffle maker until medium-hot. Pour in just enough batter to fill about two-thirds full. Close lid and cook for 3 minutes or until no longer steaming. Repeat with remaining batter.

Crêpes Suzette

*Soaked in orange and
brandy, then flamed at the
table, these crêpes are sure
to impress your guests.
Only you need know how
simple they are to prepare!*

TIP

Make the crêpes ahead,
wrap and freeze. When
ready to use, thaw while
still wrapped as you
prepare the sauce.

VARIATION

Any orange liqueur can
be used in this recipe –
Grand Marnier, Cointreau
or Triple Sec.

SIX-INCH (15 CM) CRÊPE PAN OR FRYPAN, LIGHTLY GREASED

CRÊPES

2/3 cup	all-purpose flour	150 mL
2 tsp	granulated sugar	10 mL
1/4 tsp	salt	1 mL
2/3 cup	milk	150 mL
1/3 cup	water	75 mL
1 tbsp	melted butter	15 mL
2	eggs	2

ORANGE SAUCE

1/2 cup	butter	125 mL
1/2 cup	frozen orange juice concentrate, thawed	125 mL
4 tsp	granulated sugar	20 mL
4 oz	orange liqueur	125 mL
2 oz	brandy	50 mL

1. Crêpes: In a large bowl, stir together flour, sugar and salt.

2. In a small bowl, whisk together milk, water, melted butter and eggs. Pour mixture over dry ingredients all at once, stirring until smooth. Cover and refrigerate for at least 1 hour or preferably overnight. Bring batter back to room temperature before using.

3. Heat pan until medium-hot. Add 3 tbsp (45 mL) batter for each crêpe, tilting and rotating pan to ensure batter covers entire bottom of pan. Cook for 1 1/2 to 2 minutes or until the edges begin to brown. Turn carefully with a non-metal spatula or fingertips. Cook for another 30 to 45 seconds. Remove to a plate and repeat with remaining batter.

4. **Sauce:** In a frypan or crêpe pan, melt butter and orange juice. Stir in sugar and orange liqueur. Add crêpes, one at a time, spoon sauce over crêpe until well saturated. Gently fold crêpe in half and then in quarters. Gently remove to a heatproof dish. Repeat with remaining crêpes. Pour any remaining sauce over crêpes. Warm the brandy, add to crêpes in dish and flame. Serve 2 to 3 crêpes to each person.

Multigrain Pancake and Waffle Mix

MAKES 7 CUPS (1.75 L)

With this mix on hand, you'll always be ready to whip up a batch of pancakes in a hurry.

TIP

For added convenience, use resealable storage bags to package this mix in single-recipe quantities.

Store in an airtight container in a cool, dry place or freezer for 6 months.

VARIATION

Substitute 2/3 cup (150 mL) whole wheat flour, 1/3 cup (75 mL) multigrain cereal and 1/3 cup (75 mL) flaxseeds for the multigrain flour.

2 cups	whole wheat flour	500 mL
1 cup	all-purpose flour	250 mL
1 cup	multigrain flour	250 mL
1 cup	quick-cooking oats	250 mL
1/2 cup	nonfat or skim milk powder	125 mL
1/4 cup	granulated sugar	50 mL
2 tsp	baking powder	10 mL
1 tsp	baking soda	5 mL
1/2 tsp	salt	2 mL

1. In a very large bowl, stir together whole wheat flour, flour, multigrain flour, oats, milk powder, sugar, baking powder, baking soda and salt. (See Tip, at left, for storage instructions.)

Applesauce Pancakes

**MAKES FIVE
4-INCH (10 CM) PANCAKES**

TIP

No need to peel the apple; the skins soften as they cook.

VARIATION

Diced peach, plum or pear can replace the apple.

Dice extra fruit, warm in the microwave, and use to garnish pancakes.

LIGHTLY GREASED FRYPAN OR GRILL

1 cup	Pancake and Waffle Mix (see recipe, page 92)	250 mL
1/3 cup	diced apples	75 mL
1	egg	1
1 tbsp	vegetable oil	15 mL
3/4 cup	unsweetened applesauce	175 mL

1. In a bowl stir together Pancake and Waffle Mix with apples.

2. In a bowl whisk together egg, oil and applesauce. Pour mixture over dry ingredients all at once, stirring with a few quick strokes, just until combined.

3. Heat frypan or grill until medium-hot. Pour in about 1/4 cup (50 mL) for each pancake. When the under-side is brown and the bubbles begin to break on the surface, turn and cook about 30 to 60 seconds longer or until the second side is golden brown.

Banana Blueberry Pancakes

**MAKES FIVE
4-INCH (10 CM) PANCAKES**

*Bananas and blueberries
make a great combination
in these pancakes – even
better when served with
warm blueberry sauce.*

TIP

Add 2 tsp (10 mL) orange
or lemon zest to give an
extra flavor boost to
these pancakes.

VARIATION

For an "all-banana" ver-
sion, omit the blueberries
and add extra sliced
banana.

LIGHTLY GREASED FRYPAN OR GRILL

1 1/4 cups	Pancake and Waffle Mix (see recipe, page 92)	300 mL
1	egg	1
1 tbsp	vegetable oil	15 mL
1 cup	mashed ripe banana	250 mL
1/3 to 1/2 cup	frozen blueberries	75 to 125 mL

1. In a bowl measure Pancake and Waffle Mix.

2. In another bowl, whisk together egg, oil and banana.
Add mixture to dry ingredients all at once, stirring with a
few quick strokes, just until combined.

3. Heat frypan or grill until medium-hot. Pour in about
1/4 cup (50 mL) for each pancake. Sprinkle each with
1 to 2 tbsp (15 to 25 mL) blueberries. When the under-
side is brown and the bubbles begin to break on the
surface, turn and cook about 30 to 60 seconds longer
or until the second side is golden brown.

Multigrain Nut Pancakes

**MAKES FIVE
4-INCH (10 CM) PANCAKES**

*Crunchy walnuts make a
surprising and tasty
addition to these pancakes.*

TIP

If the batter is too thick,
add another 1 to 2 tbsp
(15 to 25 mL) water.

VARIATION

Substitute pecans or
flaxseeds for the walnuts.

LIGHTLY GREASED FRYPAN OR GRILL

1 1/4 cups	Pancake and Waffle Mix (see recipe, page 92)	300 mL
1/2 cup	chopped walnuts	125 mL
3/4 cup	water	150 mL
1	egg	1
1 tbsp	vegetable oil	15 mL

1. In a bowl stir together Pancake and Waffle Mix with walnuts.

2. In another bowl, whisk together water, egg and oil. Pour mixture over dry ingredients all at once, stirring with a few quick strokes, just until combined.

3. Heat frypan or grill until medium-hot. Pour in about 1/4 cup (50 mL) for each pancake. When the underside is brown and the bubbles begin to break on the surface, turn and cook about 30 to 60 seconds longer or until the second side is golden brown.

Multigrain Waffles

**MAKES THREE
7-INCH (17.5 CM) WAFFLES**

WAFFLE MAKER, LIGHTLY GREASED

1 1/4 cups	Pancake and Waffle Mix (see recipe, page 92)	300 mL
3/4 cup	water	175 mL
2	eggs, separated	2
2 tbsp	vegetable oil	15 mL

TIP

For information about preheating waffle maker, see Techniques Glossary, page 185.

For instructions on how to whip egg whites to stiff peaks, see Techniques Glossary, page 185.

VARIATION

Try sprinkling a few frozen blueberries on the batter in the waffle maker, just before closing the top.

1. In a bowl measure Pancake and Waffle Mix.

2. In another bowl, whisk together egg yolks, oil and water. Pour mixture over dry ingredients all at once, stirring with a few quick strokes, just until combined.

3. In a separate small bowl, using an electric mixer, beat egg whites until stiff but not dry peaks form; fold into batter. Mixture should be lumpy.

4. Heat waffle maker until medium-hot. Pour in just enough batter to fill about two-thirds full. Close lid and cook for 3 minutes or until no longer steaming. Repeat with remaining batter.

Sweet Treats

P erfect for dessert – or any time you crave a little sweetness in your day – these breads are irresistible. From the tangy sweetness of lemon and coconut to the decadent richness of white chocolate and crunchy macadamia nuts, here are flavors you'll love.

SHARING THE SWEETNESS

Sweet loaves are ideal for bazaars and bake sales, or as gifts for new neighbors. Here's how you can share the breads you bake for your family.

Any batter in this chapter (or others in the book) can be divided equally between smaller pans, using the equivalencies shown below. Just be sure each pan is about three-quarters full. Pan measurements are taken across the inside top.

For each 9- by 5- by 3-inch (2 L) pan, you can use:

- One 8- by 4- by 3-inch (1.5 L) pan
- Two 7 1/2- by 3 1/2- by 2 1/2-inch (1 L) pans
- Two or three 5 3/4- by 3 1/4- by 2 1/2-inch (500 mL) pans
- Six 4 1/2- by 2 1/2- by1 1/2-inch (250 mL) pans
- Twelve 2 1/2 inch (7 cm) muffin cups

When baking in smaller pans, you should use the same temperature as with the larger loaves (the exception being muffins, which should be baked at 375° F [190° C]), but you will require less baking time. Remember, too, that the material from which the loaf pan is made (light or dark metal, glass, nonstick, etc.) will have a considerable effect on baking times. Loaves in thin, disposable pans require far less time to bake than heavier, metal pans. In each case, it makes sense to watch the loaves closely.

Handle single-use aluminum baking pans carefully. Support the bottom when moving batter-filled pans. They collapse when lifted from the sides.

GREAT GIFT IDEAS

- Wrap a loaf in aluminum foil, then in a square of cellophane or colorful nylon net (tulle) large enough to gather over the loaf. Tie with a large bow or curling ribbon.

- Bake 3 or 4 different loaves. Arrange 2 or 3 slices of each on an attractive serving plate. Wrap in plastic wrap. Purchase one-of-a-kind plates at local antique or garage sales. The plate becomes part of the gift.

- For school fund raisers, bake loaves in disposable aluminum pans. Wrap and send (in the pan) with your child to school. Attach an ingredient list or the recipe in case of allergies.

- When a friend has brought you a casserole or a pie for a neighborhood get-together, return the plate with an attractive arrangement of different quick breads. It's a great way to say "thank you!"

Apricot Date Loaf

MAKES 1 LOAF

PREHEAT OVEN TO 350° F (180° C)
9- BY 5-INCH (2 L) LOAF PAN, LIGHTLY GREASED

This tangy, moist loaf combines the wonderfully complementary flavors of sweet dates and tart dried apricots.

2 cups	all-purpose flour	500 mL
3/4 cup	graham wafer crumbs	175 mL
1/2 cup	granulated sugar	125 mL
1 tbsp	baking powder	15 mL
1/2 tsp	salt	2 mL
1 tbsp	grated orange zest	15 mL
1/2 cup	chopped dried apricots (see Tip, at left)	125 mL
1/2 cup	chopped dates	125 mL
2 tbsp	vegetable oil	25 mL
2	eggs	2
1 1/2 cups	plain yogurt	375 mL

TIP

Use scissors to snip the dried apricots into small pieces.

VARIATION

Instead of plain, use apricot-flavored yogurt – regular, low-fat or fat-free.

1. In a large bowl, stir together flour, graham wafer crumbs, sugar, baking powder, salt and zest. Stir in dried apricots and dates.

2. In a separate bowl, using an electric mixer, beat oil, eggs and yogurt until combined. Pour mixture over dry ingredients and stir just until combined. Spoon into prepared pan.

3. Bake in preheated oven for 70 to 80 minutes or until a cake tester inserted in the center comes out clean. Let cool in pan on rack for 10 minutes. Remove from pan and let cool completely on rack.

Apricot Orange Bread

MAKES 1 LOAF

PREHEAT OVEN TO 350° F (180° C)
9- BY 5-INCH (2 L) LOAF PAN, LIGHTLY GREASED

Perfect to pack for school (or office) lunches, this quick bread is moist, but not too sweet, with the sunny goodness of orange and apricot in combination with the tang of yogurt.

TIP

Use scissors to snip the dried apricots into long, thin slivers.

VARIATION

Substitute ground cinnamon or cloves for the nutmeg.

2 cups	all-purpose flour	500 mL
1/2 cup	granulated sugar	125 mL
1 1/2 tsp	baking powder	7 mL
1/2 tsp	baking soda	2 mL
1/2 tsp	salt	2 mL
2 tbsp	grated orange zest	25 mL
1 tsp	ground nutmeg	5 mL
1 cup	slivered dried apricots (see Tip, at left)	250 mL
2 tbsp	vegetable oil	25 mL
2	eggs	2
1 1/4 cups	plain yogurt	300 mL

1. In a large bowl, stir together flour, sugar, baking powder, baking soda, salt, zest and nutmeg. Stir in dried apricots.

2. In a separate bowl, using an electric mixer, beat oil, eggs and yogurt until combined. Pour mixture over dry ingredients and stir just until combined. Spoon into prepared pan.

3. Bake in preheated oven for 70 to 80 minutes or until a cake tester inserted in the center comes out clean. Let cool in pan on rack for 10 minutes. Remove from pan and let cool completely on rack.

Blueberry Banana Oat Bread

MAKES 1 LOAF

PREHEAT OVEN TO 350° F (180° C)
9- BY 5-INCH (2 L) LOAF PAN, LIGHTLY GREASED

This blueberry-studded loaf is sure to please even the most discriminating palates. For a more pronounced banana flavor, serve warm from the oven.

TIP

Leave blueberries in the freezer until just before using. This will help to prevent them from "bleeding" into the bread.

Use ripe bananas for the best flavor.

VARIATION

Try natural wheat bran instead of the oat bran.

1 3/4 cups	all-purpose flour	425 mL
1/4 cup	quick-cooking oats	50 mL
2 tbsp	oat bran	25 mL
1/2 cup	granulated sugar	125 mL
2 tsp	baking powder	10 mL
1/2 tsp	salt	2 mL
2 tbsp	vegetable oil	25 mL
1	egg	1
1 1/2 cups	mashed bananas	375 mL
3/4 cup	frozen blueberries (see Tip, at left)	175 mL

1. In a large bowl, stir together flour, oats, oat bran, sugar, baking powder and salt.

2. In a separate bowl, using an electric mixer, beat oil, egg and banana until combined. Pour mixture over dry ingredients and stir just until combined. Gently fold in frozen blueberries. Spoon into prepared pan.

3. Bake in preheated oven for 70 to 80 minutes or until a cake tester inserted in the center comes out clean. Let cool in pan on rack for 10 minutes. Remove from pan and serve warm.

Buttermilk Chocolate Orange Loaf

MAKES 1 LOAF

PREHEAT OVEN TO 350° F (180° C)
9- BY 5-INCH (2 L) LOAF PAN, LIGHTLY GREASED

Who can resist the combination of chocolate and orange? The buttermilk brings out the chocolate flavor without adding a lot of calories.

TIP

The chocolate pieces will partially melt or remain whole, depending on whether you use mini chips, regular-size chips or chocolate chunks.

VARIATION

Instead of regular chocolate, try raspberry- or mint-flavored chocolate chips.

2 cups	all-purpose flour	500 mL
1/3 cup	granulated sugar	75 mL
1/4 cup	unsweetened cocoa	50 mL
2 tsp	baking powder	10 mL
1 tsp	baking soda	5 mL
1/2 tsp	salt	2 mL
2 tbsp	grated orange zest	25 mL
2/3 cup	mini chocolate chips	150 mL
1/4 cup	vegetable oil	50 mL
2	eggs	2
2/3 cup	buttermilk	150 mL
2/3 cup	fresh orange juice	150 mL

1. In a large bowl, stir together flour, sugar, cocoa, baking powder, salt and zest. Stir in chocolate chips.

2. In a separate bowl, using an electric mixer, beat oil, eggs, buttermilk and orange juice until combined. Pour mixture over dry ingredients and stir just until combined. Spoon into prepared pan.

3. Bake in preheated oven for 50 to 60 minutes or until a cake tester inserted in the center comes out clean. Let cool in pan on rack for 10 minutes. Remove from pan and let cool completely on rack.

Chocolate Chip Loaf

MAKES 1 LOAF

Serve this not-too-sweet loaf with a glass of milk for a perfect after-school snack.

TIP

If you want the chips to soften and partially melt, use the mini-chips called for in this recipe.

VARIATION

Instead of chocolate chips, try butterscotch or peanut butter chips.

PREHEAT OVEN TO 350° F (180° C)
9- BY 5-INCH (2 L) LOAF PAN, LIGHTLY GREASED

2 cups	all-purpose flour	500 mL
1/2 cup	granulated sugar	125 mL
1 tbsp	baking powder	15 mL
1/2 tsp	salt	2 mL
2/3 cup	mini chocolate chips	150 mL
1/4 cup	vegetable oil	50 mL
1	egg	1
1 cup	milk	250 mL
1/2 tsp	vanilla extract	2 mL

1. In a large bowl, stir together flour, sugar, baking powder and salt. Stir in chocolate chips.

2. In a separate bowl, using an electric mixer, beat oil, egg, milk and vanilla extract until combined. Pour mixture over dry ingredients and stir just until combined. Spoon into prepared pan.

3. Bake in preheated oven for 50 to 60 minutes or until a cake tester inserted in the center comes out clean. Let cool in pan on rack for 10 minutes. Remove from pan and let cool completely on rack.

Chocolate Zucchini Bread

MAKES 1 LOAF

Who would have thought chocolate could be so healthy? No one will guess there are vegetables hidden in this loaf!

TIP

There's no need to peel the zucchini – just wash, dry and shred in a food processor or by hand. Drain any accumulated liquid (but do not squeeze dry) before adding to the other ingredients.

VARIATION

Instead of regular chocolate, try raspberry-flavored or white chocolate chips.

PREHEAT OVEN TO 350° F (180° C)
9- BY 5-INCH (2 L) LOAF PAN, LIGHTLY GREASED

2 cups	all-purpose flour	500 mL
1/2 cup	granulated sugar	125 mL
1/4 cup	unsweetened cocoa	50 mL
1 tbsp	baking powder	15 mL
1/2 tsp	baking soda	2 mL
1/2 tsp	salt	2 mL
1 tbsp	grated orange zest	15 mL
1/2 tsp	ground ginger	2 mL
1 cup	mini chocolate chips	250 mL
1 cup	shredded zucchini (see Tip, at left)	250 mL
1/4 cup	vegetable oil	50 mL
1	egg	1
3/4 cup	unsweetened applesauce	175 mL

1. In a large bowl, stir together flour, sugar, cocoa, baking powder, baking soda, salt, zest and ginger. Stir in chocolate chips and zucchini.

2. In a separate bowl, using an electric mixer, beat oil, egg and applesauce until combined. Pour mixture over dry ingredients and stir just until combined. Spoon into prepared pan.

3. Bake in preheated oven for 60 to 70 minutes or until a cake tester inserted in the center comes out clean. Let cool in pan on rack for 10 minutes. Remove from pan and let cool completely on rack.

Glazed Lemon Coconut Bread

MAKES 1 LOAF

PREHEAT OVEN TO 350° F (180° C)
9- BY 5-INCH (2 L) LOAF PAN, LIGHTLY GREASED

Make this delightfully sweet tea bread ahead, then freeze, so its ready to serve the next time a friend drops in. Defrost individually wrapped slices in the microwave.

TIP

Use either desiccated or shredded coconut in this recipe.

If using sweetened coconut, decrease the sugar by 1 or 2 tbsp (15 or 25 mL).

VARIATION

For a milder flavor replace lemon juice and zest with orange.

2 1/4 cups	all-purpose flour	550 mL
1 cup	granulated sugar	250 mL
1 tbsp	baking powder	15 mL
1/4 tsp	salt	1 mL
1 tbsp	grated lemon zest	15 mL
3/4 cup	unsweetened coconut (see Tip, at left)	175 mL
2 tbsp	vegetable oil	25 mL
2	eggs	2
3/4 cup	milk	175 mL
1/4 cup	lemon juice	50 mL

LEMON GLAZE

1 cup	confectioners (icing) sugar	250 mL
1/4 cup	fresh lemon juice	50 mL

1. In a large bowl, stir together flour, sugar, baking powder, salt and zest. Stir in coconut.

2. In a separate bowl, using an electric mixer, beat oil, eggs and milk until combined. Stir in lemon juice. Pour mixture over dry ingredients and stir just until combined. Spoon into prepared pan.

3. Bake in preheated oven for 70 to 80 minutes or until a cake tester inserted in the center comes out clean. Meanwhile prepare glaze.

4. **Glaze:** In a small bowl, combine confectioners (icing) sugar and lemon juice. With a long wooden skewer, poke several holes through the hot cake as soon as it is removed from the oven. Spoon the glaze over hot loaf. Allow cake to cool in pan on rack for 30 minutes. Remove from pan and let cool completely before serving.

Macadamia White Chocolate Chip Bread

MAKES 1 LOAF

PREHEAT OVEN TO 350° F (180° C)

9- BY 5-INCH (2 L) LOAF PAN, LIGHTLY GREASED

This decadent loaf oozes with pockets of melted chocolate, yet it isn't too sweet. Just try to resist tasting before it cools!

TIP

Don't chop the macadamia nuts too finely or you'll lose the crunchy texture.

VARIATION

This loaf is just about perfect the way it is. However, you could try adding 1 tbsp (15 mL) orange zest for a slightly different flavor.

1 3/4 cups	all-purpose flour	425 mL
1/2 cup	packed brown sugar	125 mL
2 tsp	baking powder	10 mL
1/2 tsp	salt	2 mL
3/4 cup	white chocolate chips	175 mL
1/2 cup	chopped macadamia nuts (see Tip, at left)	125 mL
1/4 cup	vegetable oil	50 mL
1	egg	1
1 cup	milk	250 mL

1. In a large bowl, stir together flour, brown sugar, baking powder and salt. Stir in chocolate chips and macadamia nuts.

2. In a separate bowl, using an electric mixer, beat oil, egg and milk until combined. Pour mixture over dry ingredients and stir just until combined. Spoon into prepared pan.

3. Bake in preheated oven for 70 to 80 minutes or until a cake tester inserted in the center comes out clean. Let cool in pan on rack for 10 minutes. Remove from pan and serve warm, or allow to cool completely on rack.

Morning Glory Bread

MAKES 2 LOAVES

With so many wonderfully fresh ingredients in this recipe, you have to make two loaves – one to enjoy now, and the other to share with neighbors or to freeze for company.

TIP

Be sure you don't drain the pineapple; just spoon juice and pulp into your measuring cup.

VARIATION

Make this recipe using four or five 5 3/4- by 3 1/4- by 2 1/2-inch (500 mL) mini pans. Wrap with ribbon for Christmas gifts.

PREHEAT OVEN TO 350° F (180° C)
TWO 9- BY 5-INCH (2 L) LOAF PANS, LIGHTLY GREASED

3 3/4 cups	all-purpose flour	925 mL
1/2 cup	granulated sugar	125 mL
2 tsp	baking powder	10 mL
2 tsp	baking soda	10 mL
1 1/2 tsp	salt	7 mL
1 tsp	ground cinnamon	5 mL
2 cups	shredded carrots	500 mL
1/3 cup	vegetable oil	75 mL
2	eggs	2
2 cups	unsweetened applesauce	500 mL
1 cup	crushed pineapple, with juice (see Tip, at left)	250 mL
3/4 cup	unsweetened coconut	175 mL
1/2 cup	raisins	125 mL

1. In a large bowl, stir together flour, sugar, baking powder, baking soda, salt and cinnamon. Stir in carrots.

2. In a separate bowl, using an electric mixer, beat oil, eggs and applesauce until combined. Stir in pineapple. Pour mixture over dry ingredients and stir just until combined. Stir in coconut and raisins. Spoon into prepared pans.

3. Bake in preheated oven for 70 to 80 minutes or until a cake tester inserted in the center comes out clean. Let cool in pan on rack for 10 minutes. Remove from pan and let cool completely on rack.

Nutmeg Sour Cream Bread

MAKES 1 LOAF

PREHEAT OVEN TO 350° F (180° C)
9- BY 5-INCH (2 L) LOAF PAN, LIGHTLY GREASED

Flecks of brown nutmeg stand out against a snow-white background in this tangy-sweet loaf. It makes a great accompaniment to almost anything.

TIP

Be sure to mix only until moist; otherwise the loaf will be tough and flavorless.

For best flavor, use freshly grated whole nutmeg. Use approximately half as much fresh grated as ground.

2 1/4 cups	all-purpose flour	550 mL
1/2 cup	granulated sugar	125 mL
2 tsp	baking powder	10 mL
1/2 tsp	baking soda	2 mL
1/2 tsp	salt	2 mL
1 tsp	ground nutmeg	5 mL
2 tbsp	vegetable oil	25 mL
1	egg	1
1 1/2 cups	sour cream	375 mL

1. In a bowl stir together flour, sugar, baking powder, baking soda, salt and nutmeg.

2. In a separate bowl, using an electric mixer, beat oil, egg and sour cream until combined. Pour mixture over dry ingredients and stir just until combined. Spoon into prepared pan.

3. Bake in preheated oven for 70 to 80 minutes or until a cake tester inserted in the center comes out clean. Let cool in pan on rack for 10 minutes. Remove from pan and let cool completely on rack.

Nutty Mocha Java Loaf

MAKES 1 LOAF

PREHEAT OVEN TO 350° F (180° C)
9- BY 5-INCH (2 L) LOAF PAN, LIGHTLY GREASED

Here's the ultimate dessert combo – chocolate, coffee, orange and hazelnuts – all in one delectable loaf!

TIP

Don't chop the hazelnuts too finely, or you'll lose the crunchy texture.

For instructions on removing hazelnut skins, see Techniques glossary, page 183.

VARIATION

Use any coffee liqueur (such as Tia Maria or Baileys Irish Cream) or substitute thawed frozen orange juice concentrate.

2 cups	all-purpose flour	500 mL
2 tbsp	unsweetened cocoa	25 mL
2 tbsp	baking powder	25 mL
1/2 tsp	salt	2 mL
1 tbsp	grated orange zest	15 mL
1/2 cup	chopped hazelnuts (see Tip, at left)	125 mL
1/4 cup	vegetable oil	50 mL
2	eggs	2
1 cup	coffee (at room temperature)	250 mL
1 tbsp	coffee liqueur	15 mL
1/2 cup	corn syrup	125 mL

1. In a large bowl, stir together flour, cocoa, baking powder, salt and zest. Stir in hazelnuts.

2. In a separate bowl, using an electric mixer, beat oil, eggs, coffee and liqueur until combined. Add corn syrup while mixing. Pour mixture over dry ingredients and stir just until combined. Spoon into prepared pan.

3. Bake in preheated oven for 70 to 80 minutes or until a cake tester inserted in the center comes out clean. Let cool in pan on rack for 10 minutes. Remove from pan and let cool completely on rack.

Orange Streusel Loaf

MAKES 1 LOAF

What an attractive, tasty treat! The crunchy streusel topping contrasts beautifully with the bright orange interior of this bread.

TIP

Remove the bread carefully from the pan or the topping will shake off.

VARIATION

Add 2 or 3 tbsp (25 or 45 mL) finely chopped nuts to the topping.

PREHEAT OVEN TO 350° F (180° C)

9- BY 5-INCH (2 L) LOAF PAN, LIGHTLY GREASED

STREUSEL TOPPING

1/4 cup	packed brown sugar	50 mL
1 tbsp	all-purpose flour	15 mL
1/2 tsp	ground cinnamon	2 mL
1 tbsp	melted butter	15 mL

QUICK BREAD

2 cups	all-purpose flour	500 mL
1/2 cup	granulated sugar	125 mL
2 tsp	baking powder	10 mL
1/4 tsp	baking soda	1 mL
1/2 tsp	salt	2 mL
2 tbsp	grated orange zest	25 mL
1/4 cup	vegetable oil	50 mL
2	eggs	2
3/4 cup	fresh orange juice	175 mL

1. **Streusel Topping:** In a bowl combine brown sugar, flour and cinnamon. Add butter and mix until crumbly; set aside.

2. **Quick Bread:** In a large bowl, stir together flour, sugar, baking powder, baking soda, salt and zest.

3. In a separate bowl, using an electric mixer, beat oil, eggs and orange juice until combined. Pour mixture over dry ingredients and stir just until combined. Spoon into prepared pan. Sprinkle streusel topping over batter just before baking.

4. Bake in preheated oven for 70 to 80 minutes or until a cake tester inserted in the center comes out clean. Let cool in pan on rack for 10 minutes. Carefully remove from pan and let cool completely on rack.

Prune and Apricot Bread

MAKES 1 LOAF

<small>PREHEAT OVEN TO 350° F (180° C)</small>
<small>9- BY 5-INCH (2 L) LOAF PAN, LIGHTLY GREASED</small>

While this bread is more compact than most, it is packed with deliciously moist fruit.

1/2 cup	whole wheat flour	125 mL
1 1/4 cups	all-purpose flour	300 mL
1/3 cup	packed brown sugar	75 mL
2 tsp	baking powder	10 mL
1/2 tsp	baking soda	2 mL
1/4 tsp	salt	1 mL
1/2 cup	chopped dried apricots	125 mL
1/2 cup	chopped pitted prunes	125 mL
1/2 cup	raisins	125 mL
1/4 cup	vegetable oil	50 mL
2	eggs	2
2/3 cup	orange juice	150 mL

TIP

Instead of chopping with a knife, snip dried apricots and prunes with kitchen shears. Dip blades in hot water when they become sticky.

VARIATION

Try using chopped dates instead of the prunes or raisins.

1. In a large bowl, stir together whole wheat flour, all-purpose flour, brown sugar, baking powder, baking soda and salt. Stir in apricots, prunes and raisins.

2. In a separate bowl, using an electric mixer, beat oil, eggs and orange juice until combined. Pour mixture over dry ingredients and stir just until combined. Spoon into prepared pan.

3. Bake in preheated oven for 70 to 80 minutes or until a cake tester inserted in the center comes out clean. Let cool in pan on rack for 10 minutes. Remove from pan and let cool completely on rack.

Sticky Bun Loaf

MAKES 1 LOAF

The next time you have a yearning for sticky buns – but no time to wait for dough to rise – try this quick and easy recipe!

TIP

Heat corn syrup in an ovenproof glass liquid measuring cup.

For easier pouring, microwave the corn syrup for the glaze for 50 seconds on High.

VARIATION

Add some raisins and substitute walnuts and raisins for the pecans in the topping.

Make this recipe as a coffee cake: Spread Pecan Topping in a lightly greased 9-inch (2.5 L) baking pan. Spoon quick bread batter over the topping. Bake in preheated oven for 30 to 35 minutes or until a cake tester inserted in the center comes out clean. Immediately turn upside down on a serving platter. Drizzle with warm corn syrup glaze.

PREHEAT OVEN TO 350° F (180° C)
9- BY 5-INCH (2 L) LOAF PAN, LIGHTLY GREASED

PECAN TOPPING

1 cup	coarsely chopped pecans	250 mL
1/2 cup	packed brown sugar	125 mL
1/4 cup	all-purpose flour	50 mL
2 tsp	ground cinnamon	10 mL
1/4 cup	melted butter	50 mL

QUICK BREAD

1 3/4 cups	all-purpose flour	425 mL
1/2 cup	granulated sugar	125 mL
1 1/2 tsp	baking powder	7 mL
1/2 tsp	salt	2 mL
3 tbsp	vegetable oil	45 mL
2	eggs	2
1 cup	buttermilk	250 mL

CORN SYRUP GLAZE

1/2 cup	warmed corn syrup	125 mL

1. **Pecan Topping:** In a small bowl, combine pecans, brown sugar, flour and cinnamon. Add melted butter and mix well; set aside.

2. **Quick Bread:** In a large bowl, stir together flour, sugar, baking powder and salt.

3. In a separate bowl, using an electric mixer, beat oil, eggs and buttermilk until combined. Pour mixture over dry ingredients and stir just until combined. Sprinkle half of pecan topping in bottom of prepared pan. Spoon two-thirds of the batter on top of pecan topping. Sprinkle with remaining pecan topping. Spoon remaining batter over topping.

4. Bake in preheated oven for 70 to 80 minutes or until a cake tester inserted in the center comes out clean. Immediately turn upside down on a serving platter. Drizzle with warmed corn syrup glaze.

Tangy Lemon Blueberry Almond Bread

MAKES 1 LOAF

PREHEAT OVEN TO 350° F (180° C)
9- BY 5-INCH (2 L) LOAF PAN, LIGHTLY GREASED

As its name promises, this loaf delivers an extra-refreshing burst of lemon flavor in every bite.

TIP

Leave blueberries in the freezer until just before using. This will help to prevent them from "bleeding" into the bread.

Keep a lemon in the freezer. Zest while frozen, then juice after warming in the microwave.

VARIATION

Substitute frozen cranberries for the blueberries and walnuts or pecans for the almonds.

1 cup	whole wheat flour	250 mL
1 cup	all-purpose flour	250 mL
1/2 cup	granulated sugar	125 mL
2 tsp	baking powder	10 mL
1/2 tsp	salt	2 mL
2 tbsp	grated lemon zest	25 mL
2/3 cup	slivered almonds	150 mL
1/3 cup	vegetable oil	75 mL
2	eggs	2
2/3 cup	milk	150 mL
1/3 cup	fresh lemon juice	75 mL
3/4 cup	frozen blueberries	175 mL

1. In a large bowl, stir together whole wheat flour, flour, sugar, baking powder, salt and zest. Stir in almonds.

2. In a separate bowl, using an electric mixer, beat oil, eggs and milk until combined. Add lemon juice while mixing. Pour mixture over dry ingredients and stir just until combined. Gently fold in frozen blueberries. Spoon into prepared pan.

3. Bake in preheated oven for 70 to 80 minutes or until a cake tester inserted in the center comes out clean. Let cool in pan on rack for 10 minutes. Remove from pan and let cool completely on rack.

Yogurt Plum Bread

MAKES 1 LOAF

TIP

For attractive contrasts in color and flavor, use both yellow and dark plums.

Four medium plums yield 1 cup (250 mL) chopped.

VARIATION

Try apricot- or peach-flavored yogurt (regular, low-fat or fat-free) instead of the plain variety.

PREHEAT OVEN TO 350° F (180° C)
9- BY 5-INCH (2 L) LOAF PAN, LIGHTLY GREASED

2 cups	all-purpose flour	500 mL
1/4 cup	granulated sugar	50 mL
2 tsp	baking powder	10 mL
1/2 tsp	baking soda	2 mL
1/2 tsp	salt	2 mL
1 tbsp	grated orange zest	15 mL
3 tbsp	vegetable oil	45 mL
2	eggs	2
2/3 cup	plain yogurt	150 mL
2 cups	chopped fresh plums	500 mL

1. In a large bowl, stir together flour, sugar, baking powder, baking soda, salt and zest.

2. In a separate bowl, using an electric mixer, beat oil, eggs and yogurt until combined. Pour mixture over dry ingredients and stir just until combined. Gently fold in plums. Spoon into prepared pan.

3. Bake in preheated oven for 70 to 80 minutes or until a cake tester inserted in the center comes out clean. Let cool in pan on rack for 10 minutes. Remove from pan and let cool completely on rack.

All the Flavor Without the Fat

Fat-free and low-fat breads needn't be tough and flavorless. By adding fruit purées or corn syrup, you get a moist, sweet loaf with an attractive brown crust. Try these recipes – they're low in fat, high in fiber, and packed with nutritious fruits and interesting grains.

TIPS AND TECHNIQUES FOR REDUCING FAT

Fat has a bad reputation among health-conscious people these days, but it still serves a number of important functions in baking. It is fat that creates a moist, tender crumb and a light product. It adds flavor and enhances browning, and helps to retain freshness.

Still, too much fat is bad for you. So the challenge for contemporary bakers is to find ways to reduce the fat, while keeping as many of its benefits as possible.

Fat can be cut in half for most older recipes without any major problems, although the final product will tend to dry out more quickly than regular recipes. To prevent this, we need to find ingredients that add or retain water. Fruit purées (such as applesauce, mashed banana, pear, pumpkin, prune or fig) work well, since they add moisture. Their natural sugar content also helps browning.

Here are some other suggestions for reducing the fat content of baked goods:

For recipes containing higher-fat sour cream, you can safely substitute no-fat yogurt or puréed low-fat cottage cheese.

Instead of greasing pans with butter, shortening, oil or margarine, spray them with vegetable spray. This prevents baked goods from sticking while adding virtually no extra fat.

Corn syrup is another good fat substitute. It creates a moist texture and intensifies the flavor of the other ingredients. Interestingly enough, the loaf is no sweeter than loaves prepared with sugar or honey.

When baking low-fat loaves, you may need to reduce the oven temperature and shorten the baking time slightly to prevent excess drying. Once baked, enjoy them quickly (we don't think this will be too difficult!). Store in an airtight container for a few days or freeze for longer periods.

Low-Fat Applesauce Raisin Bread

MAKES 1 LOAF

PREHEAT OVEN TO 350° F (180° C)
9- BY 5-INCH (2 L) LOAF PAN, LIGHTLY GREASED

This bread is so moist and flavorful, you'll never guess it contains no added fat.

TIP

Instead of using egg whites, try using 1 whole egg. This will increase the fat content slightly, but yields a softer textured loaf.

VARIATION

Substitute dates for raisins and ground ginger or nutmeg for the cinnamon.

2 cups	all-purpose flour	500 mL
1/2 cup	granulated sugar	125 mL
1 tsp	baking powder	5 mL
1/2 tsp	baking soda	2 mL
1/4 tsp	salt	1 mL
1/2 tsp	ground cinnamon	2 mL
1 cup	raisins	250 mL
2	egg whites	2
1 1/4 cups	unsweetened applesauce	300 mL

1. In a large bowl, stir together flour, sugar, baking powder, baking soda, salt and cinnamon. Stir in raisins.

2. In a separate bowl, using an electric mixer, beat egg whites and applesauce until combined. Pour mixture over dry ingredients and stir just until combined. Spoon into prepared pan.

3. Bake in preheated oven for 70 to 80 minutes or until a cake tester inserted in the center comes out clean. Let cool in pan on rack for 10 minutes. Remove from pan and let cool completely on rack.

Low-Fat Banana Multigrain Loaf

MAKES 1 LOAF

PREHEAT OVEN TO 350° F (180° C)

9- BY 5-INCH (2 L) LOAF PAN, LIGHTLY GREASED

Moist, delicious, nutritious and low in fat – this loaf is also full of fiber. What more could anyone want?

TIP

Typical for a banana bread, this loaf is slightly darker at the bottom than at the top.

Mash and freeze ripe bananas so they are ready when you need them for baking.

Use quick-cooking (not instant) oats.

VARIATION

Add 1/2 cup (125 mL) raisins, nuts or dates.

1 1/4 cups	all-purpose flour	300 mL
1/2 cup	bran cereal	125 mL
1/2 cup	quick-cooking oats	125 mL
1/3 cup	7-grain cereal	75 mL
1/3 cup	packed brown sugar	75 mL
1 tsp	baking powder	5 mL
1 tsp	baking soda	5 mL
1/2 tsp	salt	2 mL
2	egg whites	2
2/3 cup	skim or nonfat milk	150 mL
1/3 cup	corn syrup	75 mL
2 tbsp	molasses	25 mL
1 cup	mashed banana	250 mL

1. In a large bowl, stir together flour, bran cereal, oats, 7-grain cereal, brown sugar, baking powder, baking soda and salt.

2. In a separate bowl, using an electric mixer, beat egg whites, milk, corn syrup, molasses and banana until combined. Pour mixture over dry ingredients and stir just until combined. Spoon into prepared pan.

3. Bake in preheated oven for 70 to 80 minutes or until a cake tester inserted in the center comes out clean. Let cool in pan on rack for 10 minutes. Remove from pan and let cool completely on rack.

Blueberry Buckwheat Bread

MAKES 1 LOAF

PREHEAT OVEN TO 350° F (180° C)
9- BY 5-INCH (2 L) LOAF PAN, LIGHTLY GREASED

Soft and moist, dark and blue, this bread is delicious – and nutritious too!

TIP

Leave blueberries in the freezer until just before using. This will help to prevent them from "bleeding" into the bread.

VARIATION

Try substituting half or all of the blueberries with frozen sour cherries or cranberries.

1 2/3 cups	all-purpose flour	400 mL
1/3 cup	buckwheat flour	75 mL
1 tbsp	baking powder	15 mL
1/2 tsp	salt	2 mL
1 tsp	grated lemon zest	5 mL
3 tbsp	vegetable oil	45 mL
2	egg whites	2
1 1/4 cups	plain yogurt	300 mL
1/3 cup	honey	75 mL
1/2 cup	frozen blueberries	125 mL

1. In a large bowl, stir together flour, buckwheat flour, baking powder, salt and zest.

2. In a separate bowl, using an electric mixer, beat oil, eggs, yogurt and honey until combined. Pour mixture over dry ingredients and stir just until combined. Gently fold in frozen blueberries. Spoon into prepared pan.

3. Bake in preheated oven for 70 to 80 minutes or until a cake tester inserted in the center comes out clean. Let cool in pan on rack for 10 minutes. Remove from pan and let cool completely on rack.

Low-Fat Cornmeal Bread

MAKES 1 LOAF

This cornbread doesn't need fat to create its beautifully moist texture. It makes an attractive contrast when served with slices of a darker loaf such as MARITIME MOLASSES DATE BRAN LOAF (see recipe, page 31).

TIP

The batter in this recipe is thicker than most, but still bakes into a moist, tender quick bread.

VARIATION

For a different texture, try using a coarser grind of yellow cornmeal.

For a spicier, more flavorful loaf, add chives, chili peppers or Parmesan cheese. Serve warm for best flavor.

PREHEAT OVEN TO 350° F (180° C)
9- BY 5-INCH (2 L) LOAF PAN, LIGHTLY GREASED

1 1/2 cups	all-purpose flour	375 mL
1 cup	cornmeal	250 mL
2 tsp	baking powder	10 mL
1/2 tsp	salt	2 mL
2	egg whites	2
2 tbsp	honey	25 mL
1	can (14 oz [398 mL]) cream-style corn	1

1. In a large bowl, stir together flour, cornmeal, baking powder and salt.

2. In a separate bowl, using an electric mixer, beat egg whites and honey until combined. Stir in corn. Pour mixture over dry ingredients and stir just until combined. Spoon into prepared pan.

3. Bake in preheated oven for 70 to 80 minutes or until a cake tester inserted in the center comes out clean. Let cool in pan on rack for 10 minutes. Remove from pan and serve warm.

Low-Fat Date Orange Bread

MAKES 1 LOAF

PREHEAT OVEN TO 350° F (180° C)
9- BY 5-INCH (2 L) LOAF PAN, LIGHTLY GREASED

As attractive as it is healthy, this golden, date-studded loaf is unbelievably moist and flavorful.

TIP

Here we use corn syrup to replace the fat, supplying extra moisture to keep the loaf fresh longer.

Be sure to use fresh orange juice and zest. The flavor makes all the difference.

VARIATION

Substitute lemon for the orange zest and 1/4 cup (50 mL) each lemon juice and water for the orange juice.

1/2 cup	boiling water	125 mL
1 cup	coarsely chopped dates	250 mL
2 cups	all-purpose flour	500 mL
1/3 cup	granulated sugar	75 mL
1 tsp	baking powder	5 mL
1 tsp	baking soda	5 mL
1/2 tsp	salt	2 mL
2 tbsp	grated orange zest	25 mL
2	egg whites	2
1/2 cup	fresh orange juice	125 mL
1/3 cup	corn syrup	75 mL

1. In a bowl pour boiling water over dates; set aside to cool to room temperature.

2. In a large bowl, stir together, flour, sugar, baking powder, baking soda, salt and zest.

3. In a separate bowl, using an electric mixer, beat egg whites, orange juice and corn syrup until combined. Stir in reserved dates and water. Pour mixture over dry ingredients and stir just until combined. Spoon into prepared pan.

4. Bake in preheated oven for 70 to 80 minutes or until a cake tester inserted in the center comes out clean. Let cool in pan on rack for 10 minutes. Remove from pan and let cool completely on rack.

Low-Fat Herbed Beer Bread

MAKES 1 LOAF

Fat-fee and easy to prepare, this loaf has a delicate yeast flavor that works well with soups, salads and egg dishes.

TIP

Any type of beer works well in this recipe – whether cold or at room temperature, flat or foamy.

VARIATION

Increase the quantity of one dried herb to bring out the flavor you like best.

PREHEAT OVEN TO 350° F (180° C)
9- BY 5-INCH (2 L) LOAF PAN, LIGHTLY GREASED

2 3/4 cups	all-purpose flour	675 mL
2 tbsp	granulated sugar	25 mL
2 tbsp	baking powder	25 mL
1 tsp	salt	5 mL
1/2 tsp	dried marjoram	2 mL
1/2 tsp	dried oregano	2 mL
1/2 tsp	dried thyme	2 mL
Pinch	dried dill	Pinch
1	can (13 oz [355 mL]) beer	1

1. In a large bowl, stir together flour, sugar, baking powder, salt, marjoram, oregano, thyme and dill. Add beer and stir just until combined. Spoon into prepared pan.

2. Bake in preheated oven for 70 to 80 minutes or until a cake tester inserted in the center comes out clean. Let cool in pan on rack for 10 minutes. Remove from pan and serve warm.

Orange Millet Loaf

MAKES 1 LOAF

This rich, golden-colored loaf is studded with white pockets of soft millet. Combined with the refreshing flavor of orange, it's a real taste treat.

TIP

For information on cooking millet, see Techniques Glossary, page 184.

VARIATION

Substitute any variety of cooked rice for the millet.

PREHEAT OVEN TO 350° F (180° C)

9- BY 5-INCH (2 L) LOAF PAN, LIGHTLY GREASED

2 cups	all-purpose flour	500 mL
1/4 cup	packed brown sugar	50 mL
2 tsp	baking powder	10 mL
1 tsp	baking soda	5 mL
3/4 tsp	salt	4 mL
1 tbsp	grated orange zest	15 mL
1 cup	cooked millet (see Tip, at left)	250 mL
3 tbsp	vegetable oil	45 mL
3/4 cup	fresh orange juice	175 mL
1/4 cup	maple syrup	50 mL

1. In a large bowl, stir together flour, brown sugar, baking powder, baking soda, salt and zest. Fold in millet.

2. In a separate bowl, using an electric mixer, beat oil, orange juice and maple syrup until combined. Pour mixture over dry ingredients and stir just until combined. Spoon into prepared pan.

3. Bake in preheated oven for 70 to 80 minutes or until a cake tester inserted in the center comes out clean. Let cool in pan on rack for 10 minutes. Remove from pan and let cool completely on rack.

Soy Date Bread

MAKES 1 LOAF

PREHEAT OVEN TO 350° F (180° C)
9- BY 5-INCH (2 L) LOAF PAN, LIGHTLY GREASED

Forget about the many health benefits of soy – this date-sweetened loaf is just plain delicious.

TIP

Keep an eye on the clock when baking this loaf – it cooks more quickly than most quick breads.

Choose either low- or high-fat soy flour. It's available in health and bulk food stores.

VARIATION

Substitute raisins for the dates and plain yogurt for the buttermilk.

2/3 cup	whole wheat flour	150 mL
1 cup	all-purpose flour	250 mL
1/3 cup	soy flour	75 mL
2 tsp	baking powder	10 mL
1/2 tsp	baking soda	2 mL
1/2 tsp	salt	2 mL
2/3 cup	chopped dates	150 mL
2 tbsp	vegetable oil	25 mL
1	egg	1
2	egg whites	2
1 cup	buttermilk	250 mL
1/4 cup	maple syrup	50 mL

1. In a large bowl, stir together whole wheat flour, flour, soy flour, baking powder, baking soda and salt. Stir in dates.

2. In a separate bowl, using an electric mixer, beat oil, eggs, egg whites, buttermilk and maple syrup until combined. Pour mixture over dry ingredients and stir just until combined. Spoon into prepared pan.

3. Bake in preheated oven for 50 to 60 minutes or until a cake tester inserted in the center comes out clean. Let cool in pan on rack for 10 minutes. Remove from pan and let cool completely on rack.

Low-Fat Triple-Apple Oat Bread

MAKES 1 LOAF

PREHEAT OVEN TO 350° F (180° C)
9- BY 5-INCH (2 L) LOAF PAN, LIGHTLY GREASED

Here's a bread that will bring back memories of the apple harvest, as well as the comforting warmth of oatmeal enjoyed on a cool autumn morning.

TIP

One medium apple yields about 3/4 cup (175 mL) shredded or chopped apple. No need to peel; just core, then shred or chop.

VARIATION

Increase the allspice for a stronger flavor.

This recipe was tested with Granny Smith and McIntosh apples. But you can try it with Spy, Cortland or your favorite regional baking apple.

2 cups	all-purpose flour	500 mL
1 cup	quick-cooking oats	250 mL
2 tsp	baking powder	10 mL
1 1/2 tsp	baking soda	7 mL
1/2 tsp	salt	2 mL
1/2 tsp	ground allspice	2 mL
1 1/2 cups	shredded or finely chopped apples	375 mL
3	egg whites	3
3/4 cup	unsweetened apple juice	175 mL
1/2 cup	unsweetened applesauce	125 mL
1/2 cup	honey	125 mL

1. In a large bowl, stir together flour, oats, baking powder, baking soda, salt and allspice. Stir in apples.

2. In a separate bowl, using an electric mixer, beat egg whites, apple juice, applesauce and honey until combined. Pour mixture over dry ingredients and stir just until combined. Spoon into prepared pan.

3. Bake in preheated oven for 70 to 80 minutes or until a cake tester inserted in the center comes out clean. Let cool in pan on rack for 10 minutes. Remove from pan and let cool completely on rack.

Low-Fat Whole Wheat Raisin Bread

MAKES 1 LOAF

Sweet, moist, dark and delicious, this loaf is just as wholesome as its name suggests.

TIP

For a darker loaf, use a dark corn syrup.

VARIATION

Substitute chopped apricots or dates for the raisins.

For a stronger flavor, substitute molasses for the corn syrup.

PREHEAT OVEN TO 350° F (180° C)
9- BY 5-INCH (2 L) LOAF PAN, LIGHTLY GREASED

1 1/4 cups	whole wheat flour	300 mL
1 1/4 cups	all-purpose flour	300 mL
1/4 cup	granulated sugar	50 mL
2 tsp	baking powder	10 mL
1 tsp	baking soda	5 mL
1 tsp	salt	5 mL
1 cup	raisins	250 mL
1 cup	skim or nonfat milk	250 mL
1/3 cup	unsweetened applesauce	75 mL
1/3 cup	corn syrup	75 mL
1 tbsp	lemon juice	25 mL

1. In a large bowl, stir together whole wheat flour, flour, sugar, baking powder, baking soda and salt. Stir in raisins.

2. In a separate bowl, using an electric mixer, beat milk, applesauce, corn syrup and lemon juice until combined. Pour mixture over dry ingredients and stir just until combined. Spoon into prepared pan.

3. Bake in preheated oven for 70 to 80 minutes or until a cake tester inserted in the center comes out clean. Let cool in pan on rack for 10 minutes. Remove from pan and let cool completely on rack.

Gluten-Free Quick Breads

Do you have someone in your family who's allergic to the gluten in wheat flours? No need to bake separate breads – these flavorful treats will please everyone.

TIPS AND TECHNIQUES FOR GLUTEN-FREE BAKING

Every week we receive calls and letters from frustrated bakers who have a family member with an allergy to the gluten in wheat flours. This has prompted us to work with a variety of new and interesting gluten-free flour mixtures.

Our experience has shown that using combinations of flours in bread recipes works better than one gluten-free flour alone. It may seem a nuisance to measure so many small amounts, but the result makes the effort worthwhile. In order to minimize the trouble, we suggest preparing enough dry ingredients for 3 or 4 loaves, and dividing the mixture into single-recipe amounts; then packaging airtight, labeling and storing in the refrigerator.

When preparing gluten-free recipes, it is important that you thoroughly combine all the dry ingredients in a large bowl before adding liquids. The consistency of gluten-free flours is like a fine powder, so they are harder to mix with liquids and may lump.

It is the gluten in the wheat flour that gives the loaf its rounded top. So don't be surprised if gluten-free loaves are flatter or slightly smaller than regular quick breads.

Gluten-free loaves will crumble unless you add xanthan gum or guar gum to the recipe. Our recipes call for only a small amount of xanthan gum – but it is essential, so don't omit it.

To prevent gluten-free loaves from going stale too quickly, we add just a small amount (1 tsp [5 mL]) cider vinegar.

GLAZED LEMON COCONUT BREAD (PAGE 105) ➤

Gluten-Free Applesauce Raisin Loaf

MAKES 1 LOAF

PREHEAT OVEN TO 350° F (180° C)
9- BY 5-INCH (2 L) LOAF PAN, LIGHTLY GREASED

Here's a truly "everything free" bread – gluten-free, fat-free and yeast free – everything except sweetness and flavor!

TIP

For more information on gluten-free baking, see facing page.

VARIATION

Substitute prune purée for the applesauce.

1 1/3 cups	sorghum flour	325 mL
1/3 cup	bean flour	75 mL
1/3 cup	cornstarch	75 mL
1/2 cup	granulated sugar	125 mL
2 tsp	xanthan gum	10 mL
1 tsp	baking powder	5 mL
1/2 tsp	baking soda	2 mL
1/4 tsp	salt	1 mL
1/2 tsp	ground cinnamon	2 mL
1 cup	raisins	250 mL
2	egg whites	2
1 tsp	vinegar	5 mL
1 1/2 cups	unsweetened applesauce	375 mL

1. In a large bowl, stir together sorghum flour, bean flour, cornstarch, sugar, xanthan gum, baking powder, baking soda salt and cinnamon. Stir in raisins.

2. In a separate bowl, using an electric mixer, beat egg whites, vinegar and applesauce until combined. Pour mixture over dry ingredients and stir just until combined. Spoon into prepared pan.

3. Bake in preheated oven for 70 to 80 minutes or until a cake tester inserted in the center comes out clean. Let cool in pan on rack for 10 minutes. Remove from pan and let cool completely on rack.

≺ LOW-FAT TRIPLE-APPLE OAT BREAD (PAGE 125)

Gluten-Free Banana Nut Loaf

MAKES 1 LOAF

PREHEAT OVEN TO 350° F (180° C)
9- BY 5-INCH (2 L) LOAF PAN, LIGHTLY GREASED

With all the same great moist banana flavor of traditional banana nut bread, this gluten-free version is sure to please.

1 1/4 cups	rice flour	300 mL
1/2 cup	potato starch	125 mL
1/4 cup	tapioca starch	50 mL
1/2 tsp	xanthan gum	2 mL
1 tsp	baking powder	5 mL
1 tsp	baking soda	5 mL
1/4 tsp	salt	1 mL
3/4 cup	walnuts	175 mL
1/4 cup	vegetable oil	50 mL
2	eggs	2
1 tsp	cider vinegar	5 mL
1 1/4 cups	mashed bananas	300 mL
1/2 cup	honey	125 mL

TIP

Stir the dry ingredients thoroughly before adding to the liquids; the rice flour and starches in this recipe are so finely textured, they clump very easily.

VARIATION

Substitute pecans or flaxseeds for the walnuts.

Reduce rice flour to 1 cup (250 mL) and add 1/4 cup (50 mL) ground flaxseeds.

1. In a large bowl, stir together rice flour, potato starch, tapioca starch, xanthan gum, baking powder, baking soda and salt. Stir in walnuts.

2. In a separate bowl, using an electric mixer, beat oil, eggs, vinegar, bananas and honey until combined. Pour mixture over dry ingredients and stir just until combined. Spoon into prepared pan.

3. Bake in preheated oven for 60 to 70 minutes or until a cake tester inserted in the center comes out clean. Let cool in pan on rack for 10 minutes. Remove from pan and let cool completely on rack.

Gluten-Free Blueberry Buckwheat Bread

MAKES 1 LOAF

PREHEAT OVEN TO 350° F (180° C)

9- BY 5-INCH (2 L) LOAF PAN, LIGHTLY GREASED

If you enjoy blueberry buckwheat pancakes, you'll love the intriguing flavor of this dark loaf.

TIP

Stir the dry ingredients thoroughly before adding to the liquids; the rice flour and starches in this recipe are so finely textured, they clump very easily.

If using frozen blueberries, leave them in the freezer until just before using. This will help to prevent them from "bleeding" into the bread.

VARIATION

Substitute prunes, figs or plums for the blueberries.

3/4 cup	brown rice flour	175 mL
1/4 cup	buckwheat flour	50 mL
1/4 cup	potato starch	50 mL
1/4 cup	tapioca starch	50 mL
1 1/2 tsp	xanthan gum	7 mL
2 tsp	baking powder	10 mL
1 tsp	baking soda	5 mL
1/2 tsp	salt	2 mL
1/4 cup	vegetable oil	50 mL
2	eggs	2
1 tsp	cider vinegar	5 mL
1 1/4 cups	buttermilk	300 mL
1/2 cup	buckwheat honey	125 mL
1 cup	fresh or frozen blueberries (see Tip, at left)	250 mL

1. In a large bowl, stir together rice flour, buckwheat flour, potato starch, tapioca starch, xanthan gum, baking powder, baking soda and salt.

2. In a separate bowl, using an electric mixer, beat oil, eggs, vinegar and buttermilk until combined. Add honey while mixing. Pour mixture over dry ingredients and stir just until combined. Gently fold in blueberries. Spoon into prepared pan.

3. Bake in preheated oven for 60 to 70 minutes or until a cake tester inserted in the center comes out clean. Let cool in pan on rack for 10 minutes. Remove from pan and let cool completely on rack.

Gluten-Free Broccoli Cheddar Cornbread

MAKES NINE 3-INCH (7.5 CM) SQUARE PIECES

PREHEAT OVEN TO 350° F (180° C)

9-INCH (2.5 L) SQUARE PAN, LIGHTLY GREASED

This gluten-free cornbread is ideal for entertaining. Just cut into bite-size pieces and serve hot or cold as an hors d'oeuvre. It's also great for family meals.

TIP

Bake in a 2-quart (2 L) ovenproof glass casserole dish and serve hot, directly from the oven. Reduce baking temperature to 325° F (160° C).

VARIATION

Substitute chopped red bell pepper for half of the onions.

1 cup	cornmeal	250 mL
1 cup	rice flour	250 mL
1/4 cup	potato starch	50 mL
1/4 cup	tapioca starch	50 mL
1 tbsp	baking powder	15 mL
1 tsp	baking soda	5 mL
1 1/2 tsp	xanthan gum	7 mL
1/2 tsp	salt	2 mL
1 cup	chopped onions	250 mL
3/4 cup	shredded old Cheddar cheese	175 mL
1/4 cup	grated Parmesan cheese	50 mL
1 cup	broccoli florets	250 mL
3	eggs	3
1 tsp	cider vinegar	5 mL
2 tbsp	honey	25 mL
1	can (14 oz [398 mL]) cream-style corn	1

1. In a large bowl, stir together, cornmeal, rice flour, potato starch, tapioca starch, baking powder, baking soda, xanthan gum and salt. Stir in onions, Cheddar, Parmesan and broccoli.

2. In a separate bowl, using an electric mixer, beat eggs, vinegar and honey until combined. Stir in corn. Pour mixture over dry ingredients and stir just until combined. Spoon into prepared pan.

3. Bake in preheated oven for 35 to 45 minutes or until a cake tester inserted in the center comes out clean. Serve hot.

Gluten-Free Country Harvest Loaf

MAKES 1 LOAF

PREHEAT OVEN TO 350° F (180° C)
9- BY 5-INCH (2 L) LOAF PAN, LIGHTLY GREASED

Long-time readers of our previous books will know that this is one of our favorite flavor combinations – and here it's gluten-free!

TIP

To prevent seeds from becoming rancid, store in an airtight container in the refrigerator.

See page 40 for the wheat flour (non-gluten-free) version of this recipe.

VARIATION

Vary the combination of seeds used; try poppy, pumpkin or whatever type of seeds you prefer.

1 1/4 cups	rice flour	300 mL
1/3 cup	cornstarch	75 mL
1/3 cup	tapioca starch	75 mL
1 tbsp	baking powder	15 mL
1 1/2 tsp	xanthan gum	7 mL
3/4 tsp	salt	4 mL
1/3 cup	flaxseeds	75 mL
1/3 cup	sunflower seeds	75 mL
2 tbsp	sesame seeds	25 mL
1/3 cup	vegetable oil	75 mL
2	eggs	2
1 tsp	cider vinegar	5 mL
1 cup	milk	250 mL
1/2 cup	honey	125 mL

1. In a large bowl, stir together rice flour, cornstarch, tapioca starch, baking powder, xanthan gum and salt. Stir in flaxseeds, sunflower seeds and sesame seeds.

2. In a separate bowl, using an electric mixer, beat oil, eggs, vinegar and milk until combined. Add honey while mixing. Pour mixture over dry ingredients and stir just until combined. Spoon into prepared pan.

3. Bake in preheated oven for 60 to 70 minutes or until a cake tester inserted in the center comes out clean. Let cool in pan on rack for 10 minutes. Remove from pan and let cool completely on rack.

Gluten-Free Fresh Tomato Basil Drop Biscuits

MAKES FOURTEEN 2-INCH (5 CM) BISCUITS

PREHEAT OVEN TO 425° F (220° C)
BAKING SHEET, LIGHTLY GREASED

These biscuits are packed with the flavors of late summer – juicy, sweet tomatoes and the pungent fragrance of fresh basil.

TIP

In season, use garden-fresh beefsteak tomatoes. Use an Italian plum or Roma tomato at other times of the year.

For more information on baking biscuits, see page 54.

VARIATION

Substitute an equal amount of plain yogurt for the sour cream.

3/4 cup	rice flour	175 mL
1/4 cup	potato starch	50 mL
1/4 cup	tapioca starch	50 mL
2 tbsp	granulated sugar	25 mL
1 tbsp	baking powder	15 mL
1 tsp	xanthan gum	5 mL
1/4 tsp	salt	1 mL
1/4 cup	snipped fresh basil	50 mL
1/4 cup	snipped fresh chives	50 mL
1/4 cup	snipped fresh parsley	50 mL
1/4 cup	shortening	50 mL
3/4 cup	chopped fresh tomatoes (see Tip, at left)	175 mL
1/2 cup	sour cream	125 mL

1. In a large bowl, stir together rice flour, potato starch, tapioca starch, sugar, baking powder, xanthan gum, salt, basil, chives and parsley. Using a pastry blender, cut in shortening until mixture resembles coarse crumbs. Fold in tomatoes. Add sour cream all at once, stirring with a fork to make a soft, sticky dough. Drop by heaping tablespoonfuls onto prepared pan.

2. Bake in preheated oven for 12 to 15 minutes. Remove from baking sheet onto a cooling rack immediately. Serve warm.

Gluten-Free Peppered Zucchini Loaf

MAKES 1 LOAF

Confetti-like speckles of zucchini and pepper add to the moistness of this flavorful loaf. It's perfect for sandwiches or to serve along with a salad or stew.

TIP

Use red, yellow or orange bell peppers – or a combination of colors.

To increase the fiber content, leave the zucchini unpeeled.

VARIATION

For a little extra heat, substitute some chili or jalapeño pepper for a small amount of the bell peppers.

PREHEAT OVEN TO 350° F (180° C)
9- BY 5-INCH (2 L) LOAF PAN, LIGHTLY GREASED

1 cup	rice flour	250 mL
2/3 cup	tapioca starch	150 mL
1/3 cup	cornstarch	75 mL
1/4 cup	granulated sugar	50 mL
2 tsp	potato starch	10 mL
2 tsp	baking powder	10 mL
1 1/2 tsp	xanthan gum	7 mL
1/2 tsp	salt	2 mL
1/4 tsp	freshly ground black pepper	1 mL
1 cup	shredded zucchini	250 mL
1/2 cup	chopped bell peppers (see Tip, at left)	125 mL
1/4 cup	vegetable oil	50 mL
2	eggs	2
1 tsp	cider vinegar	5 mL
3/4 cup	buttermilk	175 mL

1. In a large bowl, stir together rice flour, tapioca starch, cornstarch, sugar, potato starch, baking powder, xanthan gum, salt and black pepper. Stir in zucchini and bell peppers.

2. In a separate bowl, using an electric mixer, beat oil, eggs, vinegar and buttermilk until combined. Pour mixture over dry ingredients and stir just until combined. Spoon into prepared pan.

3. Bake in preheated oven for 60 to 70 minutes or until a cake tester inserted in the center comes out clean. Let cool in pan on rack for 10 minutes. Remove from pan and let cool completely on rack.

Gluten-Free Pumpkin Seed Loaf

MAKES 1 LOAF

PREHEAT OVEN TO 350° F (180° C)

9- BY 5-INCH (2 L) LOAF PAN, LIGHTLY GREASED

Don't be put off by the long list of ingredients – nothing could be faster or easier than this gluten-free comfort food.

TIP

For more information on gluten-free baking, see page 128.

For a nuttier flavor, toast pumpkin and sunflower seeds before using. See page 184 for instructions.

VARIATION

Use pumpkin pie spice or your favorite combination of spices.

3/4 cup	bean flour	175 mL
3/4 cup	sorghum flour	175 mL
1/4 cup	cornstarch	50 mL
2/3 cup	packed brown sugar	150 mL
2 tsp	baking powder	10 mL
2 tsp	baking soda	10 mL
1 1/2 tsp	xanthan gum	7 mL
1/2 tsp	salt	2 mL
1 tsp	ground ginger	5 mL
1/2 tsp	ground nutmeg	2 mL
1/4 tsp	ground cloves	1 mL
1/3 cup	pumpkin seeds	75 mL
1/3 cup	sunflower seeds	75 mL
2	eggs	2
1 tsp	cider vinegar	5 mL
1/3 cup	vegetable oil	75 mL
1 cup	canned pumpkin purée (not pie filling)	250 mL

1. In a large bowl, stir together bean flour, sorghum flour, cornstarch, brown sugar, xanthan gum, baking powder, baking soda, salt, ginger, nutmeg and cloves. Stir in pumpkin seeds and sunflower seeds.

2. In a separate bowl, using an electric mixer, beat eggs, vinegar, oil and pumpkin purée until combined. Pour mixture over dry ingredients and stir just until combined. Spoon into prepared pan.

3. Bake in preheated oven for 60 to 70 minutes or until a cake tester inserted in the center comes out clean. Let cool in pan on rack for 10 minutes. Remove from pan and let cool completely on rack.

Gluten-Free Sticky Bun Snacking Cake

MAKES 1 LOAF

Traditional sticky buns are made with wheat flour and require a lot of patience as you wait for the dough to rise. This gluten-free version is ready in no time!

TIP

For easier pouring, microwave the corn syrup for 50 seconds on High.

VARIATION

Substitute walnuts or raisins for the pecans in the topping.

PREHEAT OVEN TO 350° F (180° C)
9-INCH (2.5 L) SQUARE PAN, LIGHTLY GREASED

PECAN TOPPING

1 cup	coarsely chopped pecans	250 mL
1/2 cup	packed brown sugar	125 mL
2 tsp	ground cinnamon	10 mL
1/4 cup	melted butter	50 mL

CAKE

1 1/4 cups	rice flour	300 mL
1/2 cup	potato starch	125 mL
1/4 cup	tapioca starch	50 mL
1/2 cup	granulated sugar	125 mL
1 tsp	baking powder	5 mL
1 tsp	baking soda	5 mL
1 1/2 tsp	xanthan gum	7 mL
1/4 tsp	salt	1 mL
1/4 cup	vegetable oil	50 mL
2	eggs	2
1 tsp	cider vinegar	5 mL
1 1/4 cups	yogurt	300 mL
1/2 cup	warmed corn syrup	125 mL

1. **Pecan Topping:** In a small bowl, combine pecans, brown sugar and cinnamon. Add melted butter and mix well; spread in prepared pan.

2. **Cake:** In a large bowl, stir together rice flour, potato starch, tapioca starch, sugar, baking powder, baking soda, xanthan gum and salt.

3. In a separate bowl, using an electric mixer, beat oil, eggs, vinegar and yogurt until combined. Pour mixture over dry ingredients and stir just until combined. Spoon over topping in prepared pan.

4. Bake in preheated oven for 30 to 35 minutes or until a cake tester inserted in the center comes out clean. Immediately turn upside down on a serving platter. Drizzle with warm corn syrup.

Gluten-Free Swedish Limpa

MAKES 1 LOAF

The traditional Scandinavian flavor combination of anise, caraway and fennel seed gives this orange-scented loaf a unique flavor.

TIP

For a smoother texture, use a food mill to grind the seeds.

VARIATION

Vary the combination of seeds; try poppy or sesame or your whatever type of seeds you like.

For a milder-flavored version of this loaf, omit the seeds.

PREHEAT OVEN TO 350° F (180° C)
9- BY 5-INCH (2 L) LOAF PAN, LIGHTLY GREASED

2/3 cup	bean flour	150 mL
1/2 cup	potato starch	125 mL
1/2 cup	sorghum flour	125 mL
1/2 cup	tapioca starch	125 mL
1/2 cup	packed brown sugar	125 mL
2 tsp	baking powder	10 mL
2 tsp	xanthan gum	10 mL
3/4 tsp	salt	4 mL
1 tbsp	grated orange zest	15 mL
2 tsp	anise seeds	10 mL
2 tsp	caraway seeds	10 mL
2 tsp	fennel seeds	10 mL
1/4 cup	vegetable oil	50 mL
2	eggs	2
1 tsp	cider vinegar	5 mL
1 1/4 cups	milk	300 mL

1. In a large bowl, stir together bean flour, potato starch, sorghum flour, tapioca starch, brown sugar, baking powder, xanthan gum, salt and orange zest. Stir in anise seeds, caraway seeds and fennel seeds.

2. In a separate bowl, using an electric mixer, beat oil, eggs, vinegar and milk until combined. Pour mixture over dry ingredients and stir just until combined. Spoon into prepared pan.

3. Bake in preheated oven for 60 to 70 minutes or until a cake tester inserted in the center comes out clean. Let cool in pan on rack for 10 minutes. Remove from pan and let cool completely on rack.

Super Fast and Easy Quick Breads

There are quick breads – and then there are *really* quick breads. By preparing your own mixes in advance, or using a commercial mix, you can enjoy all the goodness of home baking in just a fraction of the time!

TIPS FOR MAKING YOUR OWN MIXES

Store mixes in an airtight container at room temperature or in the freezer.

Label and date the mix before storing – it's easy to forget which mix is which. We add the page number of the recipe to the label so it's easy to find the directions for preparation.

Stir mixes thoroughly before using; otherwise, heavier ingredients (such as grains and seeds) may settle to the bottom.

Thaw frozen mixes and allow to warm to room temperature before measuring and using.

USING COMMERCIAL MIXES

Be sure to use the package size called for in the recipe. If you use too much (or too little), the product won't bake in the time specified by the recipe.

Use a fork to mash or break up any lumps in the mix before adding liquids.

When using a commercial mix in one of our recipes, ignore any instructions on the box (such as those specifying the addition of water or eggs). The recipe will identify all the ingredients you need, as well as the preparation method necessary to bake the loaf successfully.

Quick Bread Mix

2 cups	whole wheat flour	500 mL
7 cups	all-purpose flour	1.75 L
1 1/2 cups	packed brown sugar	375 mL
3/4 cup	nonfat dry milk or skim milk powder	175 mL
5 tsp	baking powder	25 mL
5 tsp	baking soda	25 mL
2 tsp	salt	5 mL
3 tbsp	ground cinnamon	45 mL
1/2 tsp	ground allspice	2 mL
1/2 tsp	ground cloves	2 mL
1/2 tsp	ground ginger	2 mL

TIP

Count out loud as you measure the 7 cups (1.75 L), one at a time, using a dry ingredient measure. It is easy to get distracted and miss one.

For added convenience, divide the mix into one-loaf amounts and keep in resealable storage bags.

VARIATION

Feel free to vary the amount of spices – or omit them entirely – according to your personal taste.

1. In a very large bowl, stir together whole wheat flour, flour, brown sugar, milk powder, baking powder, baking soda, salt and spices. Mix well.

2. Store dry mix in an airtight container at room temperature for up to 6 weeks or in the freezer for up to 6 months.

Banana Flaxseed Quick Bread

MAKES 1 LOAF

PREHEAT OVEN TO 350° F (180° C)

9- BY 5-INCH (2 L) LOAF PAN, LIGHTLY GREASED

Banana and flaxseeds make a great partnership in this bread, with each flavor complementing the other.

3 1/4 cups	Quick Bread Mix (see recipe, page 141)	800 mL
1/2 cup	flaxseeds	125 mL
1/3 cup	vegetable oil	75 mL
2	eggs	2
1 1/2 cups	mashed banana	375 mL
1/2 cup	water	125 mL

TIP

Stir the mix before spooning lightly into dry measures. Do not pack.

VARIATION

Raisins or nuts can be substituted for the flaxseeds.

1. In a large bowl, stir together quick bread mix and flaxseeds.

2. In a separate bowl, using an electric mixer, beat oil, eggs, mashed banana and water until combined. Pour mixture over dry ingredients and stir just until combined. Spoon into prepared pan.

3. Bake in preheated oven for 60 to 70 minutes or until a cake tester inserted in the center comes out clean. Immediately invert on a cooling rack. Remove pan and let cool completely.

Cranberry Applesauce Quick Bread

MAKES 1 LOAF

PREHEAT OVEN TO 350° F (180° C)
9- BY 5-INCH (2 L) LOAF PAN, LIGHTLY GREASED

With this colorful loaf, there's no easier way to enjoy the sweetness of raisins and applesauce with the contrasting tart- ness of cranberries.

TIP

Stir the mix before spooning lightly into dry measures. Do not pack.

VARIATION

Add 1/2 cup (125 mL) of your favorite kind of nuts or substitute them for the raisins; replace water with cranberry-apple juice.

3 1/4 cups	Quick Bread Mix (see recipe, page 141)	800 mL
1/2 cup	raisins	125 mL
1/3 cup	vegetable oil	75 mL
2	eggs	2
1 1/2 cups	unsweetened applesauce	375 mL
1/2 cup	water	125 mL
1/2 cup	frozen or fresh cranberries	125 mL

1. In a large bowl, stir together quick bread mix and raisins.

2. In a separate bowl, using an electric mixer, beat oil, eggs, applesauce and water until combined. Pour mixture over dry ingredients and stir just until combined. Gently fold in frozen cranberries. Spoon into prepared pan.

3. Bake in preheated oven for 60 to 70 minutes or until a cake tester inserted in the center comes out clean. Immediately invert on a cooling rack. Remove pan and let cool completely.

Pineapple Nut Quick Bread

MAKES 1 LOAF

PREHEAT OVEN TO 350° F (180° C)

9- BY 5-INCH (2 L) LOAF PAN, LIGHTLY GREASED

The natural sweetness of the pineapple, along with the moist texture it provides, makes this an excellent addition to any lunch bag.

3 1/4 cups	Quick Bread Mix (see recipe, page 141)	800 mL
1/2 cup	chopped walnuts	125 mL
1/3 cup	vegetable oil	75 mL
2	eggs	2
1/2 cup	pineapple juice (see Tip, at left)	125 mL
1 1/2 cups	drained crushed pineapple	375 mL

TIP

Drain the juice from the pineapple into a measuring cup. If necessary, add water to make up the 1/2 cup (125 mL) called for in the recipe.

VARIATION

For a different flavor, add 1/2 cup (125 mL) shredded carrots or coconut.

1. In a large bowl, stir together quick bread mix and walnuts.

2. In a separate large bowl, using an electric mixer, beat oil, eggs and juice until combined. Pour mixture over dry ingredients and stir just until combined. Spoon into prepared pan. Fold in pineapple.

3. Bake in preheated oven for 60 to 70 minutes or until a cake tester inserted in the center comes out clean. Immediately invert on a cooling rack. Remove pan and let cool completely.

Pumpkin Pecan Quick Bread

MAKES 1 LOAF

PREHEAT OVEN TO 350° F (180° C)
9- BY 5-INCH (2 L) LOAF PAN, LIGHTLY GREASED

Looking for a change from traditional pumpkin pies at Thanksgiving? Try this loaf.

TIP

Stir mix before spooning lightly into dry measures. Do not pack.

Toast the pumpkin seeds and pecans for a more intense flavor. See page 184 for instructions.

VARIATION

For a spicier loaf, add traditional pumpkin pie spices – ground ginger, nutmeg and cloves.

3 1/4 cups	Quick Bread Mix (see recipe, page 141)	800 mL
1/4 cup	pumpkin seeds (see Tip, at left)	50 mL
1/4 cup	chopped pecans	50 mL
1/3 cup	vegetable oil	75 mL
2	eggs	2
1 cups	canned pumpkin purée (not pie filling)	250 mL
1/2 cup	water	125 mL

1. In a large bowl, stir together quick bread mix, pumpkin seeds and pecans.

2. In a separate bowl, using an electric mixer, beat oil, eggs, pumpkin purée and water until combined. Pour mixture over dry ingredients and stir just until combined. Spoon into prepared pan.

3. Bake in preheated oven for 60 to 70 minutes or until a cake tester inserted in the center comes out clean. Immediately invert on a cooling rack. Remove pan and let cool completely.

Buttermilk Biscuit Mix

*Hot buttermilk biscuits –
what a special treat for
dinnertime! With this mix
you can whip them up in
just a few minutes;
they bake while you
make the salad. (See
Traditional Buttermilk
Biscuits, page 149.)*

TIP

For added convenience,
divide the mix into one-loaf
amounts and keep in
resealable storage bags.

For more information on
baking biscuits, see
page 54.

2 cups	whole wheat flour	500 mL
6 cups	all-purpose flour	1.5 L
1 1/4 cups	buttermilk powder	300 mL
1/4 cup	granulated sugar	50 mL
1/4 cup	baking powder	50 mL
2 tsp	cream of tartar	10 mL
1 tsp	baking soda	5 mL
1 1/2 tsp	salt	7 mL
2 1/3 cups	shortening	575 mL

1. In a very large bowl, stir together whole wheat flour,
flour, buttermilk powder, sugar, baking powder, cream
of tartar, baking soda and salt. Using a pastry blender,
cut in shortening until mixture resembles coarse crumbs.

2. Store mix in an airtight container in a cool, dry place.
Or freeze for up to 6 months.

Cheese Biscuits

**MAKES THIRTEEN
2-INCH (5 CM) BISCUITS**

PREHEAT OVEN TO 425° F (220° C)
BAKING SHEET, LIGHTLY GREASED

*These biscuits need only
10 minutes to bake – but
their wonderful aroma will
make that seem like an
eternity!*

TIP

For information on
weight/volume equivalents
of cheese, see page 178.

VARIATION

Add 2 to 3 tbsp (25 to
45 mL) fresh dill or snipped
chives to the dry mix.

2 cups	Buttermilk Biscuit Mix (see recipe, page 146)	500 mL
3/4 cup	shredded old Cheddar cheese	175 mL
1/4 cup	grated Parmesan cheese	50 mL
1/2 cup	water	125 mL

1. In a large bowl, stir together biscuit mix, Cheddar and Parmesan cheeses. Add water all at once, stirring with a fork to make a soft, but slightly sticky dough.

2. With lightly floured hands, form dough into a ball. On a lightly floured surface, knead the dough gently for 8 to 10 times. Pat or roll out the dough into a 3/4-inch (2 cm) thick round.

3. Using a 2-inch (5 cm) floured cutter, cut out as many rounds as possible. Place on prepared baking sheet. Gently form scraps into a ball, flatten and cut out rounds.

4. Bake in preheated oven for 10 to 12 minutes. Remove from baking sheet onto a cooling rack immediately. Serve warm.

Pumpkin Ginger Mini-Scones

MAKES 3 1/2 DOZEN MINI-SCONES

Enjoy these bite-size treats with leftover turkey and cranberries on the day after Thanksgiving.

TIP

For even faster preparation, make regular-size scones. Follow the method for CHEESE BISCUITS (see recipe, page 147).

VARIATION

Substitute leftover mashed squash for the pumpkin purée and grated ginger root for the crystallized ginger.

PREHEAT OVEN TO 425° F (220° C)
BAKING SHEET, LIGHTLY GREASED

2 2/3 cups	Buttermilk Biscuit Mix (see recipe, page 146)	650 mL
1/4 cup	chopped crystallized ginger	50 mL
3/4 cup	canned pumpkin purée (not pie filling)	175 mL
1/4 cup	milk	50 mL

1. In a large bowl, stir together biscuit mix and crystallized ginger.

2. In a small bowl, stir together pumpkin purée and milk. Add pumpkin mixture all at once, stirring with a fork to make a soft, but slightly sticky dough.

3. With lightly floured hands, form dough into a ball. On a lightly floured surface, knead the dough gently for 8 to 10 times. Pat or roll out the dough into a 1/2-inch (1 cm) round.

4. Using a 1 3/8-inch (3 cm) floured cutter, cut out as many rounds as possible. Place on prepared baking sheet. Gently form scraps into a ball, flatten and cut out rounds.

5. Bake in preheated oven for 10 to 12 minutes. Remove from baking sheet onto a cooling rack immediately. Serve warm.

Traditional Buttermilk Biscuits

MAKES 8 BISCUITS

PREHEAT OVEN TO 425° F (220° C)
BAKING SHEET, LIGHTLY GREASED

2 1/3 cups	Buttermilk Biscuit Mix (see recipe, page 146)	575 mL
1/2 cup	water	125 mL

M-M-M good! There's nothing that reminds us more of grandmother's kitchen than hot buttermilk biscuits served hot from the oven on a brisk winter afternoon.

TIP

For light, flaky biscuits, try to handle the dough as little as possible.

VARIATION

For a "drop biscuit" version of this recipe, add an extra 2 to 3 tbsp (25 to 45 mL) water to the dough mixture. No need to knead and roll out, just drop by large heaping spoonfuls onto the prepared baking sheet.

1. In a large bowl, combine biscuit mix and water, stirring with a fork to make soft but slightly sticky dough.

2. With lightly floured hands, form dough into a ball. On a lightly floured surface, knead the dough gently for 8 to 10 times. Pat or roll out the dough into a 1/2-inch (2 cm) thick round.

3. Using a 3-inch (7.5 cm) floured cutter, cut out as many rounds as possible. Place on prepared baking sheet. Gently form scraps into a ball, flatten and cut out rounds.

4. Bake in preheated oven for 10 to 12 minutes. Remove from baking sheet onto a cooling rack immediately. Serve hot.

Orange Date Loaf from a Mix

MAKES 1 LOAF

PREHEAT OVEN TO 350° F (180° C)
9- BY 5-INCH (2 L) LOAF PAN, LIGHTLY GREASED

Need a quick and easy loaf to take to a bake sale? This recipe is ideal.

TIP

Use half of a 1 lb 14-oz (900 g) package of commercially prepared muffin mix. Don't guess – measure out the whole package and divide into 2 equal portions. Use one and store the other in an airtight bag.

VARIATION

Any commercially prepared muffin mix can replace the low-fat bran variety. We have made this recipe with oatmeal, low-fat apple and carrot mixes – all with success.

3 cups	Low-Fat Bran Muffin mix (commercially prepared)	750 mL
1/2 cup	chopped dates	125 mL
1/2 cup	frozen orange juice concentrate, thawed	125 mL
1/4 cup	water	50 mL
1	egg	1

1. In a large bowl, stir together muffin mix and dates.

2. In a small bowl, whisk together orange juice, water and egg. Pour liquids over mix and stir just until combined. Spoon into prepared pan.

3. Bake in preheated oven for 60 to 70 minutes or until a cake tester inserted in the center comes out clean. Immediately invert on a cooling rack. Remove pan and let cool completely.

Apple Raisin Oatmeal Loaf from a Mix

MAKES 1 LOAF

PREHEAT OVEN TO 350° F (180° C)
9- BY 5-INCH (2L) LOAF PAN, LIGHTLY GREASED

With a commercial muffin mix and a few simple ingredients in your cupboard, you're always ready when you need a delicious loaf in a hurry. This one is ideal to serve as a snack or with fruit for dessert

3 cups	Oatmeal Muffin mix (commercially prepared)	750 mL
1/2 cup	raisins	125 mL
3/4 cup	unsweetened applesauce	175 mL
1	egg	1

1. In a large bowl, stir together mix and raisins.

2. In a small bowl, whisk together applesauce and egg. Pour applesauce mixture over mix and stir just until combined. Spoon into prepared pan.

3. Bake in preheated oven for 60 to 70 minutes or until a cake tester inserted in the center comes out clean. Immediately invert on a cooling rack. Remove pan and let cool completely.

TIP

Use half of a 1 lb 14 oz (900 g) package of commercially prepared muffin mix. Don't guess – measure out the whole package and divide into 2 equal portions. Use one and store the other in an airtight bag.

VARIATION

Substitute any commercially prepared muffin mix for the oatmeal. A low-fat apple or carrot mix makes a good choice.

Glazed Lemon Loaf from a Mix

MAKES 2 LOAVES

This loaf is a perennial favorite at church bake sales. It always sells quickly.

TIP

Take a little extra time to dissolve the gelatin completely, then let it cool before adding the mix.

VARIATION

Any flavor of gelatin dessert mix and pudding cake mix works well in this recipe.

PREHEAT OVEN TO 350° F (180° C)
TWO 9- BY 5-INCH (2 L) LOAF PANS, LIGHTLY GREASED

1	pkg (3 oz [85 g]) lemon gelatin dessert mix	1
1 cup	boiling water	250 mL
1	pkg (18 oz [510 g]) lemon pudding cake mix	1
1/2 cup	vegetable oil	125 mL
4	eggs	4

HOT LEMON GLAZE

1 cup	confectioners (icing) sugar	250 mL
1/4 cup	fresh lemon juice	50 mL

1. In a small bowl, add water to gelatin powder, stir until completely dissolved. Let cool to room temperature.

2. In a large bowl, using an electric mixer, combine cake mix, vegetable oil, eggs and gelatin mixture. Beat on medium speed for 2 to 3 minutes. Spoon into prepared pans.

3. Bake in preheated oven for 40 to 50 minutes or until a cake tester inserted in the center comes out clean. Meanwhile prepare the glaze.

4. **Glaze:** In a small bowl, combine confectioners sugar and lemon juice. With a long wooden skewer, poke several holes through the hot cake as soon as it is removed from the oven. Pour the glaze over hot loaves.

5. Let cool in pan on rack for 30 minutes. Remove from pan and let cool completely on rack.

Quick Breads from Your Bread Machine

Bread machines are used primarily to simplify the task of baking yeast breads. But they're also great for baking cakes and quick breads. Here are some of our favorite quick bread recipes, specially developed for your bread machine.

If your bread machine features a cycle called "Quick Bread," "Cake" or "Batter Bread," then you can use it to prepare the recipes in this chapter. ("Instant," "Rapid" or "Bake" cycles are not the same, and will not work.)

Before trying these recipes, it's important to read your bread machine manual and follow any instructions carefully. Bread machines have different characteristics – as we learned when testing recipes for this chapter, using a variety of machines, both vertical and horizontal. In some cases, the same recipe came out as a round-topped golden loaf in one machine, but would end up as a pale (although cooked), flat-topped cube when baked in another. Textures also varied widely – from fine and cake-like to more open and less tender – since some machines just gently mix then knead (thus creating finer textures), while others knead vigorously for a long time.

Other variables include length of cycle time (ranging from 1 hour and 15 minutes to just under 2 hours), as well as the ability of some machines to let you vary the loaf size, the crust color and extend the baking time. Some bread machines have a "keep warm" operation that allows the loaf to continue to bake.

With all these differences between machines, chances are you'll need to make minor adjustments in the recipes. Jot down any changes you make as you bake.

Here are a few hints for baking better quick breads using your bread machine.

• Add ingredients in the order recommended by the recipe or according to the directions given in your bread machine manual.

• To ensure even mixing and baking, all ingredients should be at room temperature or warmed according to the recipe instructions. Cut soft shortening and butter into 1-inch (2.5 cm) cubes before adding. Warm the eggs, in the shell, by placing them in a bowl of hot water for 5 minutes. Heat milk in the microwave for 1 minute on High or until room temperature. Make sure liquids do not boil.

• As soon as the machine starts to mix, scrape the corners, sides and bottom of the baking pan with a rubber or plastic spatula to make sure that all dry ingredients are incorporated and evenly mixed.

• Test for doneness with a long wooden or metal skewer before removing the quick bread from the machine and before the machine is turned off. Some quick breads must be left in the baking pan, in the bread maker, during the "keep warm" operation in order to continue to bake completely.

• If your machine does not have a "keep warm" cycle, and the quick bread is not baked at the end of the baking time, switch the bread machine to "Bake" and bake another 10 minutes. Test again and repeat this procedure if necessary.

• Cool cakes in baking pan on the cooling rack for 10 minutes before turning out to cool completely. If the cake sticks to the pan, loosen it at the corners and sides with a rubber spatula before tipping it out.

Bread Machine Apple Raisin Loaf

MAKES 1 LOAF

Start with a commercial muffin mix, then add applesauce and raisins. What could be easier?

TIP

Use half of a 1 lb 14 oz (900 g) package of commercially prepared muffin mix. Don't guess – measure out the 3 cups (750 mL) you need. We found some packages actually contained up to 6 1/2 cups (1.625 L).

VARIATION

Dates, raisins or figs can replace the raisins.

3/4 cup	unsweetened applesauce	175 mL
1	egg	1
3 cups	Low-Fat Apple Muffin mix (commercially prepared)	750 mL
1/2 cup	raisins	125 mL

1. Measure ingredients into baking pan in the order recommended by the manufacturer. Insert pan into the oven chamber. Select **Quick Bread/Cake Cycle**. Scrape sides of the baking pan and the kneading blade with a rubber spatula as soon as the mixing begins.

2. When signal sounds indicating the end of cycle, test for doneness with a wooden skewer. If baked, remove baking pan from bread machine. If not completely baked, allow to remain in bread machine on "keep warm" cycle for 10 to 30 minutes or until baked.

3. Allow to cool in baking pan, on a cooling rack, for 10 minutes. Turn cake out onto a cooling rack and allow to cool completely.

Bread Machine Banana Quick Bread

MAKES 1 LOAF

Try this old-time family favorite, updated for your bread machine. It's the perfect welcome gift for a new neighbor.

TIP

The quick bread is done when a wooden skewer inserted in the center of the loaf comes out clean.

For information on warming milk to room temperature, see page 184.

Some bread machines may require up to 60 minutes on the "keep warm" cycle before the quick bread is baked. Check the manufacturer's directions to determine the length of this cycle.

VARIATION

Substitute mini chocolate chips or slivered almonds for the walnuts.

1/4 cup	milk, warmed to room temperature	50 mL
1 cup	mashed ripe bananas	250 mL
2	eggs	2
1/2 tsp	salt	2 mL
3/4 cup	granulated sugar	175 mL
3 tbsp	vegetable oil	45 mL
2 cups	all-purpose flour	500 mL
2 tsp	baking powder	10 mL
1 tsp	baking soda	5 mL
1/2 cup	chopped walnuts	125 mL

1. Measure ingredients into baking pan in the order recommended by the manufacturer. Insert pan into the oven chamber. Select **Quick Bread/Cake Cycle**. Scrape sides of the baking pan and the kneading blade with a rubber spatula as soon as the mixing begins.

2. When signal sounds indicating the end of cycle, test for doneness with a wooden skewer before turning machine off. If baked, remove baking pan from bread machine. If not completely baked, allow to remain in bread machine on "keep warm" cycle for up to 60 minutes or until baked.

3. Allow to cool in baking pan, on a cooling rack, for 10 minutes. Turn quick bread out onto a cooling rack and allow to cool completely.

Bread Machine Bacon Cheddar Cornbread

MAKES 1 LOAF

Enjoy the comforting goodness of cornbread, accented with the complementary flavors of bacon and Cheddar.

TIP

For cheese weight/volume equivalents, see page 178.

Cheese can be cut in small cubes instead of shredding to save time.

If the loaf doesn't cook completely in your bread machine, it could be that the eggs need to be warmed before using. For information on this technique, see page 183.

VARIATION

Substitute 2 to 3 oz (50 to 75 g) diced Black Forest ham for the bacon.

1 cup	canned cream-style corn	250 mL
2	eggs	2
1/4 cup	granulated sugar	50 mL
1 cup	all-purpose flour	250 mL
3/4 cup	cornmeal	175 mL
1 tbsp	baking powder	15 mL
1/2 tsp	salt	2 mL
1/2 cup	shredded old Cheddar cheese	125 ml
5	slices crisp bacon, crumbled	5

1. Measure ingredients into baking pan in the order recommended by the manufacturer. Insert pan into the oven chamber. Select **Quick Bread/Cake Cycle**. Scrape sides of the baking pan and the kneading blade with a rubber spatula as soon as the mixing begins.

2. When signal sounds indicating the end of cycle, test for doneness with a wooden skewer before turning machine off. If baked, remove baking pan from bread machine. If not completely baked, allow to remain in bread machine on "keep warm" cycle for up to 60 minutes or until baked.

3. Allow to cool in baking pan, on a cooling rack, for 10 minutes. Turn quick bread out onto a cooling rack and allow to cool completely.

Bread Machine Country Harvest Quick Bread

MAKES 1 LOAF

Try the conventional oven-baked version, (see recipe, page 40) as well as this easy bread-machine version, and see which one is your favorite.

TIP

The quick bread is done when a wooden skewer inserted in the center of the loaf comes out clean.

VARIATION

Substitute 1 cup (250 mL) water plus 1/3 cup (75 mL) buttermilk powder for the buttermilk. Measure the buttermilk powder on top of the flour and seeds.

Vary the proportions of seeds in this recipe – or substitute other seeds that you like. Just keep the total to 3/4 cup (175 mL).

1 cup	buttermilk, warmed to room temperature	250 mL
1	egg	1
1 tsp	salt	5 mL
1/4 cup	molasses	50 mL
1/4 cup	packed brown sugar	50 mL
1/4 cup	vegetable oil	50 mL
3/4 cup	whole wheat flour	175 mL
1 cup	all-purpose flour	250 mL
2 tsp	baking powder	10 mL
1/2 tsp	baking soda	2 mL
1/4 cup	flaxseeds	50 mL
1/4 cup	sunflower seeds	50 mL
2 tbsp	poppy seeds	25 mL
2 tbsp	sesame seeds	25 mL

1. Measure ingredients into baking pan in the order recommended by the manufacturer. Insert pan into the oven chamber. Select **Quick Bread/Cake Cycle**. Scrape sides of the baking pan and the kneading blade with a rubber spatula as soon as the mixing begins.

2. When signal sounds indicating the end of cycle, test for doneness with a wooden skewer before turning machine off. If baked, remove baking pan from bread machine. If not completely baked, allow to remain in bread machine on "keep warm" cycle for up to 60 minutes or until baked.

3. Allow to cool in baking pan, on a cooling rack, for 10 minutes. Turn quick bread out onto a cooling rack and allow to cool completely.

Bread Machine
Lemon Poppy Quick Bread

MAKES 1 LOAF

A perennial favorite flavor combination lemon and poppy seeds.

TIP

For information on warming yogurt and eggs, see Techniques Glossary, pages 185 and 183, respectively.

VARIATION

Substitute double the amount of orange zest for the lemon and use orange juice for the lemon juice.

1 cup	yogurt, warmed to room temperature	250 mL
1	egg (at room temperature)	1
2 tbsp	fresh lemon juice	25 mL
1/2 tsp	salt	2 mL
1/2 cup	granulated sugar	125 mL
1/4 cup	vegetable oil	50 mL
1 3/4 cups	all-purpose flour	425 mL
2 tsp	baking powder	10 mL
1 tsp	baking soda	5 mL
1 tbsp	grated lemon zest	15 mL
1/4 cup	poppy seeds	50 mL

1. Measure ingredients into baking pan in the order recommended by the manufacturer. Insert pan into the oven chamber. Select **Quick Bread/Cake Cycle**. Scrape sides of the baking pan and the kneading blade with a rubber spatula as soon as the mixing begins.

2. When signal sounds indicating the end of cycle, test for doneness with a wooden skewer before turning machine off. If baked, remove baking pan from bread machine. If not completely baked, allow to remain in bread machine on "keep warm" cycle for up to 60 minutes or until baked.

3. Allow to cool in baking pan, on a cooling rack, for 10 minutes. Turn quick bread out onto a cooling rack and allow to cool completely.

Bread Machine Orange Date Loaf

MAKES 1 LOAF

Need a quick and easy loaf to take to a bake sale? Begin with a packaged mix and make it your own by adding flavor ingredients.

TIP

Use half of a 1 lb 14 oz (900 g) package of commercially prepared muffin mix. Don't guess – measure out the 3 cups (750 mL) you need. We found some packages actually contained up to 6 1/2 cups (1.625 L).

Store the remainder in an airtight bag.

VARIATION

Any commercially prepared muffin mix can replace the carrot variety. We have made this recipe with oatmeal, low-fat apple and bran mixes – all with success.

1/2 cup	frozen orange juice concentrate, thawed and warmed to room temperature	125 mL
1/4 cup	water	50 mL
1	egg	1
3 cups	Carrot Muffin mix (commercially prepared)	750 mL
1/2 cup	chopped dates	125 mL

1. Measure ingredients into baking pan in the order recommended by the manufacturer. Insert pan into the oven chamber. Select **Quick Bread/Cake Cycle**. Scrape sides of the baking pan and the kneading blade with a rubber spatula as soon as the mixing begins.

2. When signal sounds indicating the end of cycle, test for doneness with a wooden skewer before turning machine off. If baked, remove baking pan from bread machine. If not completely baked, allow to remain in bread machine on "keep warm" cycle for up to 60 minutes or until baked.

3. Allow to cool in baking pan, on a cooling rack, for 10 minutes. Turn quick bread out onto a cooling rack and allow to cool completely.

GLUTEN-FREE BROCCOLI CHEDDAR CORNBREAD (PAGE 132) ➤

Bread Machine Pecan Squash Quick Bread

MAKES 1 LOAF

Here's the perfect combination – warm golden squash and crunchy pecans – all made simple with your bread machine.

TIP

Use any variety of winter squash – butternut, Hubbard, acorn, buttercup or turban. Be sure you don't add butter, salt or sugar to the mashed squash.

VARIATION

Substitute mashed cooked yams, sweet potatoes or pumpkin purée for the squash.

1/3 cup	milk, warmed to room temperature	75 mL
2 cups	mashed cooked squash	500 mL
2	eggs	2
1/2 tsp	salt	2 mL
1/4 cup	granulated sugar	50 mL
3 tbsp	vegetable oil	45 mL
1 cup	whole wheat flour	250 mL
1 cup	all-purpose flour	250 mL
1 tbsp	baking powder	15 mL
1/4 tsp	baking soda	1 mL
1 tsp	ground nutmeg	5 mL
1/2 cup	chopped pecans	125 mL

1. Measure ingredients into baking pan in the order recommended by the manufacturer. Insert pan into the oven chamber. Select **Quick Bread/Cake Cycle**. Scrape sides of the baking pan and the kneading blade with a rubber spatula as soon as the mixing begins.

2. When signal sounds indicating the end of cycle, test for doneness with a wooden skewer before turning machine off. If baked, remove baking pan from bread machine. If not completely baked, allow to remain in bread machine on "keep warm" cycle for up to 60 minutes or until baked.

3. Allow to cool in baking pan, on a cooling rack, for 10 minutes. Turn quick bread out onto a cooling rack and allow to cool completely.

◄ LEMON YOGURT BISCUITS (PAGE 166) AND DATE NUT LOAF (PAGE 170)

Bread Machine Polynesian Quick Bread

MAKES 1 LOAF

Sweet and simple, this from-scratch quick bread is a snap to make in your bread machine. And there's only one pan to wash!

TIP

Use flaked, shredded or desiccated coconut; while their textures vary slightly, all work well in this recipe.

To ensure even distribution through the loaf, be sure to chop the dried cherries. If the pieces are too large, they can sink to the bottom or collect around the edges.

VARIATION

For a sweeter loaf, substitute dried cranberries for the dried cherries.

1/3 cup	shortening	75 mL
1/2 cup	granulated sugar	125 mL
2	eggs, slightly beaten	2
1 cup	crushed pineapple, with juice	250 mL
1 tsp	salt	5 mL
1 3/4 cups	all-purpose flour	425 mL
4 tsp	baking powder	20 mL
3/4 cup	chopped dried cherries	175 mL
1/2 cup	unsweetened flaked coconut	125 mL

1. Measure shortening and sugar into baking pan. Add eggs. Insert pan into the oven chamber. Select **Quick Bread/Cake Cycle**. Scrape sides of baking pan and kneading blade with a rubber spatula as soon as the mixing begins. Stop bread machine after 5 minutes of mixing. Remove baking pan from machine. Add remaining ingredients in order recommended in recipe. Insert pan into the oven chamber. Select **Quick Bread/Cake Cycle**. Scrape sides of baking pan and kneading blade with a rubber spatula as soon as the mixing begins.

2. When signal sounds indicating the end of cycle test for doneness with a wooden skewer before turning machine off. If baked, remove baking pan from bread machine. If not completely baked, allow to remain in bread machine on "keep warm" cycle for up to 60 minutes or until baked.

3. Allow to cool in baking pan, on a cooling rack, for 10 minutes. Turn quick bread out onto a cooling rack and allow to cool completely.

Bread Machine Sunshine Loaf

MAKES 1 LOAF

Need a quick dessert for unexpected dinner guests? This zesty loaf is just the thing. Serve warm with fresh fruit or ice cream.

TIP

A large package of cake mix is always useful to have on hand for last-minute emergencies.

The pudding-in-mix type of cake mix works best for this recipe.

VARIATION

Substitute 1/4 cup (50 mL) lemon juice and 3/4 cup (175 mL) water for the orange juice in the cake. Make a lemon glaze using the recipe on page 105.

1	18-oz (510 g) pkg yellow or golden cake mix (pudding-in-mix type)	1
1 cup	orange juice	250 mL
3	eggs	3
1/3 cup	vegetable oil	75 mL
1 tbsp	grated orange zest	15 mL

ORANGE SYRUP

1/2 cup	granulated sugar	125 mL
1/4 cup	orange juice	50 mL

1. Measure ingredients into baking pan in the order recommended by the manufacturer. Insert pan into the oven chamber. Select **Quick Bread/Cake Cycle**. Scrape sides of the baking pan and the kneading blade with a rubber spatula as soon as the mixing begins.

2. When signal sounds indicating the end of cycle, test for doneness with a wooden skewer before turning machine off. If baked, remove baking pan from bread machine. If not completely baked, allow to remain in bread machine on "keep warm" cycle for up to 60 minutes or until baked.

3. Orange Syrup: In a small saucepan, heat sugar and orange juice, stirring constantly, until sugar is dissolved. With a long wooden skewer, poke several holes through the loaf as soon as it is removed from the bread machine. Spoon the warm syrup over the hot quick bread. Allow to cool for 30 minutes in baking pan on a cooling rack. Turn quick bread out onto serving plate and allow to cool completely.

Bread Machine Tutti-Fruiti Loaf

MAKES 1 LOAF

Chockfull of mixed candied fruit and peel, this loaf is an old favorite.
For an extra-special treat, drizzle with lemon glaze (see recipe, page 105) and serve in thin slices.

TIP

For information on warming orange juice and eggs, see page 184.

VARIATION

Turn this recipe into a Russian Kulich: Substitute part of the fruit with the same amount of raisins and toasted almonds.

Replace 1/4 cup (50 mL) of the orange juice with the same amount of thawed frozen cranberry juice concentrate.

1 1/4 cups	orange juice (at room temperature)	300 mL
1	egg (at room temperature)	1
1/2 tsp	salt	2 mL
1/3 cup	granulated sugar	75 mL
1/4 cup	vegetable oil	50 mL
2 1/4 cups	all-purpose flour	550 mL
2 tsp	baking powder	10 mL
1 tsp	baking soda	5 mL
1 cup	mixed candied fruit and peel	250 mL

1. Measure ingredients into baking pan in the order recommended by the manufacturer. Insert pan into the oven chamber. Select **Quick Bread/Cake Cycle**. Scrape sides of the baking pan and the kneading blade with a rubber spatula as soon as the mixing begins.

2. When signal sounds indicating the end of cycle, test for doneness with a wooden skewer before turning machine off. If baked, remove baking pan from bread machine. If not completely baked, allow to remain in bread machine on "keep warm" cycle for up to 60 minutes or until baked.

3. Allow to cool in baking pan, on a cooling rack, for 10 minutes. Turn quick bread out onto a cooling rack and allow to cool completely.

Grandma's Favorites Updated

Only a few generations ago, commercially prepared foods were rare, and baking was a daily necessity. From those days long past, when the smell of fresh-baked bread filled every kitchen, we have searched out old family recipes and updated them for today's home bakers.

Lemon Yogurt Biscuits

MAKES TWELVE 2-INCH (5 CM) BISCUITS

PREHEAT OVEN TO 425° F (220° C)
BAKING SHEET, UNGREASED

Tangy with yogurt and lemon, these biscuits remains soft and flaky even the next day. This recipe is our absolute favorite!

2 cups	all-purpose flour	500 mL
2 tbsp	granulated sugar	25 mL
1 tbsp	baking powder	15 mL
1/2 tsp	baking soda	2 mL
1/2 tsp	salt	2 mL
2 tsp	grated lemon zest	10 mL
1/3 cup	cold butter	75 mL
1 cup	plain yogurt	250 mL

TIP

Cold butter cuts better into dry ingredients than soft butter – and produces flakier biscuits. For easier handling, pre-cut the butter into 1-inch (2.5 cm) cubes.

Just before baking, sprinkle an extra 1 tbsp (15 mL) granulated sugar on top. This produces a nice golden color.

For more information on preparing biscuits, see page 54.

VARIATION

For a delicious shortcake biscuit, add an extra 1 tbsp (15 mL) granulated sugar to the dry ingredients. Top with sliced fresh strawberries, peaches or raspberries in season. Serve with whipped or Devonshire cream.

1. In a large bowl, stir together flour, sugar, baking powder, baking soda, salt and zest. Using a pastry blender, cut in butter until mixture resembles coarse crumbs. Add yogurt all at once, stirring with a fork to make a soft, but slightly sticky dough.

2. With lightly floured hands, form dough into a ball. On a lightly floured surface, knead the dough gently for 8 to 10 times. Pat or roll out the dough into a 1-inch (2.5 cm) thick round. Using a 2-inch (5 cm) floured cutter, cut out as many rounds as possible. Place on baking sheet. Gently form scraps into a ball, flatten and cut out rounds.

3. Bake in preheated oven for 12 to 15 minutes. Remove from baking sheet onto a cooling rack immediately.

California Walnut Cake

MAKES 1 LOAF

*Here's a very simple loaf –
all the better to let the
wonderful flavor of walnuts
shine through. It's a great
taste sensation for walnut
lovers, as is our Parmesan
Walnut Bread (see recipe,
page 42).*

PREHEAT OVEN TO 350° F (180° C)
9- BY 5-INCH (2 L) LOAF PAN, LIGHTLY GREASED

2 cups	all-purpose flour	500 mL
1 cup	packed brown sugar	250 mL
3/4 tsp	baking powder	4 mL
1/2 tsp	baking soda	2 mL
1/2 tsp	salt	2 mL
3/4 cup	chopped walnuts	175 mL
2 tbsp	vegetable oil	25 mL
1	egg	1
1 cup	buttermilk	250 mL

TIP

For a more intense flavor,
toast the walnuts before
using. For instructions, see
page 184.

VARIATION

Replace the buttermilk with
an equal amount of sour
milk or plain yogurt.
For instructions on souring
milk, see page 184.

1. In a large bowl, stir together flour, brown sugar, baking powder, baking soda and salt. Stir in walnuts.

2. In a separate bowl, using an electric mixer, beat oil, egg and buttermilk until combined. Pour over dry ingredients and stir just until combined. Spoon into prepared pan.

3. Bake in preheated oven for 70 to 80 minutes or until a cake tester inserted in the center comes out clean. Let cool in pan on rack for 10 minutes. Remove from pan and let cool completely on rack.

Mother's Banana Bread

MAKES 1 LOAF

PREHEAT OVEN TO 350° F (180° C)
9- BY 5-INCH (2L) LOAF PAN, LIGHTLY GREASED

Here's a recipe Donna grew up baking in her mother's kitchen during the late 1950s. We have included both the original (this page) and a more contemporary version (opposite page) which is not so sweet and rich. We have kept (but simplified) the method, since this produces the traditional soft crumb and fine texture we associate with banana breads. (Check the index for other banana breads in this book.)

2 cups	all-purpose flour	500 mL
1 tsp	baking soda	5 mL
1 tsp	salt	5 mL
1/2 cup	soft butter	125 mL
1 cup	granulated sugar	250 mL
2	eggs	2
1 cup	mashed bananas	250 mL
1/3 cup	milk	75 mL
1 tsp	vinegar	5 mL

1. Sift together flour, soda and salt. Cream butter; add sugar and cream well. Add eggs and beat well. Add bananas and blend thoroughly. Combine milk and vinegar. Add dry ingredients alternately with liquids, beginning and ending with dry. Blend well after each addition. Pour into prepared loaf pan. Bake in preheated oven for about 1 hour.

Banana Bread

MAKES 1 LOAF

PREHEAT OVEN TO 350° F (180° C)

9- BY 5-INCH (2 L) LOAF PAN, LIGHTLY GREASED

A welcome treat to serve on any occasion, this loaf is actually moister on the second day.

TIP

Mash and freeze ripe bananas so they are ready when you need them.

VARIATION

Try adding 1/2 cup (125 mL) flaxseeds to the dry ingredients in Step 1.

2 cups	all-purpose flour	500 mL
1 tsp	baking soda	5 mL
1/2 tsp	salt	2 mL
1/3 cup	milk	75 mL
1 cup	mashed banana	250 mL
1 tsp	white vinegar	5 mL
1/3 cup	soft shortening	75 mL
3/4 cup	granulated sugar	175 mL
2	eggs	2

1. In a large bowl, stir together flour, baking soda and salt.

2. In a small bowl, combine milk, banana and vinegar.

3. In a separate large bowl, using an electric mixer, cream shortening, sugar and eggs until light and fluffy. Stir in dry ingredients alternately with banana mixture, making 3 additions of dry ingredients and 2 of liquids; stir just until combined after each addition. Spoon into prepared pan.

4. Bake in preheated oven for 70 to 80 minutes or until a cake tester inserted in the center comes out clean. Let cool in pan on rack for 10 minutes. Remove from pan and let cool completely on rack.

Date Nut Loaf

MAKES 1 LOAF

PREHEAT OVEN TO 350° F (180° C)
9- BY 5-INCH (2 L) LOAF PAN, LIGHTLY GREASED

Dates and nuts are a classic combination, but we always think of them in terms of this traditional quick bread. Its moist, dark, sweet flavor is full of comfort and fond memories.

1 cup	coarsely chopped dates	250 mL
1/2 cup	chopped walnuts	125 mL
3 tbsp	shortening	45 mL
1 1/2 tsp	baking soda	7 mL
1/2 tsp	salt	2 mL
1 cup	boiling water	250 mL
2 cups	all-purpose flour	500 mL
3/4 cup	granulated sugar	175 mL
2	eggs	2
1 tsp	vanilla extract	5 mL

TIP

To save time, purchase pre-chopped dates. These are the same as regular dates, except the pieces are coated with dextrose to prevent them from clumping together.

VARIATION

Replace half the dates with the same quantity of figs.

1. In a bowl combine dates, walnuts, shortening, baking soda and salt. Pour boiling water over and set aside for 20 minutes.

2. In a large bowl, stir together flour and sugar.

3. In a separate bowl, using an electric mixer, beat eggs and vanilla extract until combined. Stir in date mixture. Pour over dry ingredients and stir just until combined. Spoon into prepared pan.

4. Bake in preheated oven for 70 to 80 minutes or until a cake tester inserted in the center comes out clean. Let cool in pan on rack for 10 minutes. Remove from pan and let cool completely on rack.

Golden Raisin Bread

MAKES 1 LOAF

Here's a recipe based on one passed down from Heather's mother. It was often the first to disappear from a plate of fruit breads.

TIP

The raisins are stirred in with the dry ingredients to coat them with flour. This helps to prevent them from sinking to the bottom of the loaf.

VARIATION

For a different flavor and texture, replace vanilla with almond extract and add 1/2 cup (125 mL) toasted slivered almonds.

PREHEAT OVEN TO 350° F (180° C)
9- BY 5-INCH (2 L) LOAF PAN, LIGHTLY GREASED

2 cups	all-purpose flour	500 mL
1/2 cup	granulated sugar	125 mL
1 tbsp	baking powder	15 mL
1/2 tsp	salt	2 mL
1 cup	golden raisins	250 mL
1/4 cup	vegetable oil	50 mL
2	eggs	2
1 cup	milk	250 mL
1 tsp	vanilla extract	5 mL

1. In a large bowl, stir together flour, sugar, baking powder and salt. Stir in raisins.

2. In a separate bowl, using an electric mixer, beat oil, eggs, milk and vanilla extract until combined. Pour over dry ingredients and stir just until combined. Spoon into prepared pan.

3. Bake in preheated oven for 70 to 80 minutes or until a cake tester inserted in the center comes out clean. Let cool in pan on rack for 10 minutes. Remove from pan and let cool completely on rack.

Lemon Loaf with Lemon Glaze

MAKES 1 LOAF

PREHEAT OVEN TO 350° F (180° C)
9- BY 5-INCH (2 L) LOAF PAN, LIGHTLY GREASED

Rich, sweet and moist, this loaf has a comforting pound-cake texture that has been pleasing families for generations. Derived from a traditional recipe, the only change we've made here is to intensify the lemon flavor by tripling the amount of zest.

1 1/2 cups	all-purpose flour	375 mL
1 tsp	baking powder	5 mL
1/2 tsp	salt	2 mL
1 tbsp	grated lemon zest	15 mL
1/2 cup	soft shortening	125 mL
1 cup	granulated sugar	250 mL
2	eggs	2
1/2 cup	milk	125 mL

HOT LEMON GLAZE

1/2 cup	granulated sugar	125 mL
1/4 cup	fresh lemon juice	50 mL

TIP

Keep a lemon in the freezer. Zest while frozen, then juice after warming in the microwave.

VARIATION

Try substituting lime for the lemon zest and juice.

1. In a bowl stir together flour, baking powder, salt and zest.

2. In a separate large bowl, using an electric mixer, cream shortening, sugar and eggs until light and fluffy. Stir in dry ingredients alternately with milk, making 3 additions of dry ingredients and 2 of milk; stir just until combined after each addition. Spoon into prepared pan.

3. Bake in preheated oven for 70 to 80 minutes or until a cake tester inserted in the center comes out clean. Meanwhile prepare the glaze.

4. Glaze: In a small bowl, combine sugar and lemon juice. Microwave on High for 30 seconds.

5. With a long wooden skewer, poke several holes through the hot cake as soon as it is removed from the oven. Pour the glaze over hot loaf. Let cool in pan on rack for 30 minutes. Remove from pan and let cool completely on rack.

Maraschino Cherry Loaf

MAKES 1 LOAF

PREHEAT OVEN TO 350° F (180° C)
9- BY 5-INCH (2 L) LOAF PAN, LIGHTLY GREASED

A classic holiday treat from the 1950s, this loaf features an attractive, pink, cake-like texture, and circles of bright red cherries. Serve it on a platter with contrasting darker fruit breads.

2 cups	all-purpose flour	500 mL
2 tsp	baking powder	10 mL
1 tsp	salt	5 mL
1/4 cup	soft butter	50 mL
3/4 cup	granulated sugar	175 mL
1	egg	1
1 1/4 cups	cherry juice + milk (see Tip, at left)	375 mL
1	8-oz (250 mL) jar red maraschino cherries, juice drained and reserved (see above), chopped or sliced	1

TIP

Drain cherries into a 2-cup (500 mL) liquid measure, then slowly add milk to make up the 1 1/4 cups (300 mL) liquid called for in the recipe.

VARIATION

Try green maraschino cherries for a change.

1. In a bowl stir together flour, baking powder and salt.

2. In a separate large bowl, using an electric mixer, cream butter, sugar and egg until light and fluffy. Stir in dry ingredients alternately with cherry juice/milk mixture, making 3 additions of dry ingredients and 2 of liquids; stir just until combined after each addition. Spoon into prepared pan.

3. Bake in preheated oven for 70 to 80 minutes or until a cake tester inserted in the center comes out clean. Let cool in pan on rack for 10 minutes. Remove from pan and let cool completely on rack.

Sugar Plum Loaf

MAKES 1 LOAF

This traditional Christmas favorite will have visions of sugar plums dancing in everyone's heads. With its colorful pockets of red, yellow, orange and green gumdrops, this loaf contains a sweet treat in every bite!

TIP

Finely sliver or slice gumdrops by snipping with kitchen shears. Take the time to carefully separate and coat each sliver of gumdrop with flour. If the pieces are too large, or not coated with flour, they will sink to the bottom of the loaf.

VARIATION

Change the color of gumdrops to suit any holiday celebration – green for St. Patrick's Day, for example, or black and orange for Halloween. Let your imagination run wild!

PREHEAT OVEN TO 350° F (180° C)
9- BY 5-INCH (2 L) LOAF PAN, LIGHTLY GREASED

2 cups	all-purpose flour	500 mL
2 1/2 tsp	baking powder	12 mL
1/2 tsp	salt	2 mL
2 cups	slivered gumdrops (assorted colors)	500 mL
1/3 cup	soft butter	75 mL
1/2 cup	granulated sugar	125 mL
2	eggs	2
1 cup	milk	250 mL

1. In a large bowl, stir together flour, baking powder and salt. Add gumdrops, separating and coating completely with flour.

2. In a separate large bowl, using an electric mixer, cream butter, sugar and eggs until light and fluffy. Using a rubber spatula, fold in dry ingredients alternately with milk, making 3 additions of dry ingredients and 2 of liquids; stir just until combined after each addition. Spoon into prepared pan.

3. Bake in preheated oven for 70 to 80 minutes or until a cake tester inserted in the center comes out clean. Let cool in pan on rack for 10 minutes. Remove from pan and let cool completely on rack.

Zucchini Bread

MAKES 1 LOAF

PREHEAT OVEN TO 350° F (180° C)
9- BY 5-INCH (2 L) LOAF PAN, LIGHTLY GREASED

There's an old piece of gardening wisdom that says, "before you plant zucchini make sure you have lots of friends!" Here's the perfect recipe to help you use up some of that zucchini crop.

TIP

When carrots and zucchini are plentiful, bake a number of these loaves to store in the freezer.

Pack tarragon tightly into a 1/4-cup (50 mL) dry measure, then transfer to a cup or glass and snip with scissors.

VARIATION

Substitute shredded cucumber for the zucchini; replace tarragon with fresh basil, oregano or marjoram.

1 cup	whole wheat flour	250 mL
3/4 cup	all-purpose flour	175 mL
2/3 cup	packed brown sugar	150 mL
2 tsp	baking powder	10 mL
1/2 tsp	salt	2 mL
2 tsp	snipped fresh tarragon	10 mL
1 cup	shredded carrots	250 mL
1 cup	shredded zucchini	250 mL
1/2 cup	sunflower seeds	125 mL
2 tbsp	vegetable oil	25 mL
1	egg	1
1/2 cup	milk	125 mL

1. In a large bowl, stir together whole wheat flour, flour, brown sugar, baking powder, salt and tarragon. Stir in carrots, zucchini and sunflower seeds.

2. In a separate bowl, using an electric mixer, beat oil, egg and milk until combined. Pour mixture over dry ingredients and stir just until combined. Spoon into prepared pan.

3. Bake in preheated oven for 70 to 80 minutes or until a cake tester inserted in the center comes out clean. Let cool in pan on rack for 10 minutes. Remove from pan and let cool completely on rack.

Baking liners. Reusable sheets of nonstick coated fiberglass. Flexible and food-safe, they are used to eliminate the need to grease and flour. Wash, rinse well and dry before storing.

Biscuit cutter. Similar to a cookie cutter, this can be made of stainless steel or other metals. It has very sharp edges, round in shape, and may have a handle. Common sizes include 1 1/2, 2, 2 3/8 and 2 1/2 inches (3.5, 5, 7.3, 7.5 cm) in diameter.

Blini pan. See Crêpe pan.

Cake tester. A thin, long, wooden or metal stick or wire attached to a handle that is used for baked products to test for doneness.

Cooling rack. Parallel and perpendicular thin bars of metal at right angles, with feet attached, used to hold hot baking up off the surface to allow cooling air to circulate.

Crêpe pan. Smooth, low, round pan with heavy bottom and sloping sides. It ranges from 5 to 7 inches (12.5 to 17.5 cm) in diameter. A blini pan is smaller than crêpe pan, typically 3 to 4 inches (7.5 to 10 cm) in diameter.

Crumb cake cups. Similar to a muffin cup liner, but larger, these 3 3/4- by 1-inch (9.5 by 2.5 cm) paper liners are used to bake miniature coffee cakes.

Grill. Heavy rack set over a heat source used to cook food.

Griddle. Flat metal surface on which food is cooked. Can be built into a stove or stand-alone.

Loaf pan. Metal container used for baking loaves. Common pan sizes are 9 by 5 inches (2 L) and 8 by 4 inches (1.5 L). Danish loaf pans measure 12 by 4 by 2 1/2 inches (30 by 10 by 6 cm).

Oven thermometer. Used to measure temperatures from 200° F to 500° F (100° C to 275° C). It either stands on or hangs from an oven rack.

Parchment paper. Heat-resistant paper similar to waxed paper, usually coated with silicon on one side; used with or as an alternative to other methods (such as applying vegetable oil or spray) to prevent baked goods from sticking to the baking pan.

Pastry blender. Used to cut fat into flour, it consists of five metal blades or wires held together by a handle.

Pastry brush. Small brush with nylon or natural bristles used to apply glazes or egg washes to dough. Wash thoroughly after each use. To store, lay flat or hang on a hook through a hole in the handle.

Pizza wheel. A large, sharp-edged wheel (without serrations) anchored to a handle. Use it to cut dough for tea biscuits, soda breads and scones.

Rolling pin. A heavy, smooth cylinder of wood, marble, plastic or metal; used to roll out dough.

Scone pan. A 9 5/8- by 1-inch round metal baking pan portioned into 8 sections; used to make scones by spooning in a drop batter.

Skewer. A long, thin stick (made of wood or metal) used in baking to test for doneness.

Spatula. A utensil with a handle and blade that can be long or short, narrow or wide, flexible or inflexible. It is used to spread, lift, turn, mix or smooth foods. Spatulas are made of metal, rubber or plastic.

Springform pan. A circular baking pan, available in a range of sizes, with a separable bottom and side. The side is removed by releasing a clamp, making the contents easy to remove.

Thermometer. Bakers use this metal-stemmed instrument to test the internal temperature of quick breads. Stem must be inserted at least 2 inches (5 cm) into the bread for an accurate reading. When quick bread is baked, it should register 210° F (100° C).

Waffle iron. See Waffle maker.

Waffle maker. An appliance used to cook waffles using either a built-in electric element or heat from a stovetop. Cooking surfaces have a plaid or honeycomb pattern. They cook both sides of the waffle at the same time.

Zester. A tool used to cut very thin strips of outer peel from citrus fruits. It has a short, flat blade tipped with five small holes with sharp edges.

Almond. Crack open the shell of an almond and you'll find an ivory-colored nut encased in a thin brown skin. With the skin removed, (for technique, see first entry on page 183), the almond is "blanched." In this form, almonds are sold whole, sliced, slivered and ground. Two cups (500 mL) almonds weigh about 12 oz (375 g).

Anise seeds/star anise. These tiny gray-green, egg-shaped seeds have a distinctive licorice flavor. Anise can also be purchased as a finely ground powder. For recipes that call for anise seeds, half the amount of anise powder can be substituted.

Asiago cheese. A pungent grayish-white hard cheese from northern Italy. Cured for more than 6 months, it's texture is ideal for grating.

Baking chips. Similar in consistency to chocolate chips, but with different flavors, such as butterscotch, peanut butter, cinnamon and lemon.

Baking powder. A chemical leavener, containing an alkali (baking soda) and an acid (cream of tartar), which gives off carbon dioxide gas under certain conditions, depending on the type of baking powder. Double-acting baking powder leavens twice, once when exposed to moisture and a second time when subjected to heat. The single-acting variety (which is used for the recipes in this book) leavens only when exposed to moisture.

Baking soda (sodium bicarbonate). A chemical leavener that gives off carbon dioxide gas in the presence of moisture – particularly acids such as lemon juice, buttermilk and sour cream. It is also one of the components of baking powder.

Barley. A cereal grain with a slightly sweet, nutty, earthy flavor and a chewy texture, sometimes ground into a flour with low gluten content. Barley in baked products adds to the starch and soluble fiber content. Barley flakes are made from the barley grain and look very similar to rolled oats.

Bean flour (chickpea, garbanzo bean, gram, Roamaon). A gluten-free flour made from cooked beans that absorbs more moisture than wheat flour. Stir with a fork before measuring to aerate.

Bell peppers. The sweet-flavored members of the capsicum family (which include chilies and other hot peppers), these peppers have a hollow interior lined with white ribs and seeds attached at the stem end. They are most commonly green, red or yellow, but can also be white or purple.

Blueberries. Wild low-bush berries are smaller than the cultivated variety, and more time-consuming to pick, but their flavor makes every minute of picking time worthwhile.

Brown sugar. A refined sugar with a coating of molasses. It can be purchased coarse or fine and comes in 3 varieties: dark, golden and light.

Buckwheat. Not related, despite its name, to wheat (which is a grain), buckwheat is the seed of a plant from the rhubarb family. Buckwheat flour is dark and strongly flavored, and is gluten-free. Roasted whole buckwheat, called Kasha, has a strong nutty flavor and chewy texture.

Bulgur. Whole-wheat kernels, with the bran layer removed, that have been cooked, dried and cracked into fragments. In quick bread recipes, it provides a nutty texture and flavor, as well as a somewhat coarse texture. Cracked wheat can be substituted for bulgur.

Butter. A spread produced from dairy fat and milk solids, butter can be used interchangeably in quick bread recipes for shortening, oil or margarine.

Buttermilk. Named for the way in which it was originally produced – that is, from milk left in the churn after the solid butter was removed – buttermilk is now made with fresh, pasteurized milk that has been cultured (or "soured") with the addition of a bacterial culture. The result is a slightly thickened dairy beverage with a salty, sour flavor similar to yogurt.

Buttermilk powder. A dry powder, low in calories, which softens the texture of a quick bread and heightens the flavor of ingredients such as chocolate. It is readily available from bulk- or health-food stores. Keep in an airtight container, since it lumps easily. To substitute for 1 cup (250 mL) fresh buttermilk, use 1 cup (250 mL) water and 1/3 cup (75 mL) buttermilk powder.

Caraway seeds. Small, crescent-shaped seeds of the caraway plant. They have a nutty, peppery, licorice-like flavor.

Cardamom. This popular spice is a member of the ginger family. A long green or brown pod contains the strong, spicy, lemon-flavored seed. Although native to India, cardamom is used in Middle Eastern, Indian and Scandinavian cooking – in the latter case, particularly for seasonal baked goods.

Cereal. Any grain that yields an edible part, such as wheat, oats, rye, rice or corn.

Cereal, 3-grain. See Red River cereal.

Cereal, 7-grain. Contains barley flakes, triticale flour, corn flakes, steel-cut oats, rye meal, cracked wheat, flax seed and hulled millet. And yes, for anyone who's counting, there are 8 ingredients, not 7!

Cereal, 12-grain. Contains triticale, steel-cut oats, barley flakes, sesame, buckwheat, rye meal, oats, corn, cracked wheat, millet, flax and sunflower seeds. Note: All multi-grain cereals can be used interchangeably in quick bread recipes.

Cheddar cheese. Always select an aged, good-quality Cheddar for bread machine recipes. (The flavor of mild or medium Cheddar is not strong enough for quick bread baking.) Weight/volume equivalents are:

4 oz (120 g) = 1 cup (250 mL) grated;
2 oz (60 g) = 1/2 cup (125 mL) grated;
1 1/2 oz (45 g) = 1/3 cup (75 mL) grated.

Clotted cream. Also known as Devonshire or Devon cream. Made from unpasteurized milk that is heated until a thick layer of cream forms. After cooling, the cream is skimmed off. It is popular in England to serve with scones for tea.

Cornmeal. The dried, ground kernels of white, yellow or blue corn. It has a gritty texture and is available in coarse, medium and fine grind. Its starchy-sweet flavor is most commonly associated with cornbread – a regional specialty of the southern United States.

Corn syrup. A thick, sweet syrup made from cornstarch, sold as clear (light) or brown (dark) varieties. The latter has caramel flavor and color added.

Cracked wheat. Similar to bulgur, for which it can be substituted in quick bread recipes, except that it is not pre-cooked and has not had the bran removed.

Cranberry. Grown in bogs on low vines, these sweet-tart berries are available fresh, frozen and dried. Fresh cranberries are available only in season – typically from mid-October until January, depending on your location – but can be frozen right in the bag. Substitute dried cranberries for sour cherries, raisins or currants.

Cream of tartar. An acidic component of baking powder, it is used to give volume and stability to beaten egg whites. Tartaric acid is a fine white crystalline powder that forms naturally during the fermentation of grape juice on the inside of wine barrels.

Currant. Similar in appearance to small, dark raisins, currants are made by drying a special seedless variety of grape. Not the same as a type of berry that goes by the same name.

Dates. The fruit of the date palm tree, dates are long and oval in shape, with a paper-thin skin that turns from green to dark brown when ripe. Eaten fresh or dried, dates have a very sweet, light-brown flesh around a long, narrow seed.

Devonshire cream. See Clotted cream.

Double-acting baking powder. See Baking powder.

Eggplant. Ranging in color and shape from dark purple and pear-like to light mauve and cylindrical, eggplant has a light, spongy flesh that, while bland on its own, is remarkable for its ability to absorb other flavors in cooking.

Evaporated milk. A milk product with 60% of the water removed. It is sterilized and canned, which gives it a cooked taste and darker color.

Fennel seeds. Small, oval, green-brown seeds with prominent ridges and a mild anise (licorice-like) flavor and aroma. Available whole or ground, they are used in Italian and Central European cookery, particularly in rye or pumpernickel breads.

Feta cheese. A crumbly, white, Greek-style cheese, with a salty, tangy flavor. Store in the refrigerator, in its brine, and drain well before using.

Fig. A pear-shaped fruit with a thick, soft skin. Eaten fresh or dried, the tan-colored sweet flesh contains many tiny edible seeds.

Filbert. See Hazelnut.

Flaxseed. Thin and oval shaped, dark brown in color, flaxseeds add a crunchy texture to quick breads. Research indicates that flaxseed can aid in lowering blood cholesterol levels. Ground flaxseed (also known as linseed) stale quickly, so purchase only the amount needed; store in the refrigerator.

Garbanzo bean flour. See Bean flour.

Garlic. An edible bulb composed of several sections (cloves), each covered with a papery skin. An essential ingredient in many styles of cooking.

Ginger. A bumpy rhizome, ivory to greenish-yellow in color, with a tan skin. *Fresh ginger root* has a peppery, slightly sweet flavor, similar to lemon and rosemary, and a pungent aroma. *Ground ginger* is made from the dried ginger root; it is spicier and not as sweet as fresh. *Crystallized or candied ginger* is made from pieces of fresh ginger root that have been cooked in sugar syrup and coated with sugar.

Gluten. A natural protein in wheat flour that becomes elastic with the addition of moisture and kneading. Gluten traps gases produced by leaveners inside the dough and causes it to rise.

Golden raisins. See Raisins.

Granulated sugar. A refined, crystalline, white form of sugar that is also commonly referred to as "table sugar" or just "sugar."

Hazelnut. Also known as filberts, hazelnuts have a rich, sweet, flavor that complements ingredients such as coffee and chocolate. Remove the bitter brown skin before using.

Hazelnut liqueur. The most common type is Frangelico, which is made in Italy.

Herbs. Plants whose stems, leaves or flowers are used as a flavoring, either dried or fresh. (See also individual herbs.) To substitute fresh herbs for dried, a good rule of thumb is to use three times the amount of fresh as dried. Taste and adjust the amount to suit your preference.

Honey. Sweeter than sugar, honey is available in liquid, honeycomb and creamed varieties. Use liquid honey for quick bread recipes.

Kasha. See Buckwheat.

Linseed. See Flaxseed (ground).

Macadamia nuts. The small, white, round nut of an Australian evergreen tree with a rich, buttery, slightly sweet flavor. Usually sold shelled, since they have an extremely hard shell.

Maple syrup. A very sweet, slightly thick brown liquid made by boiling the sap from North American maple trees.

Margarine. A solid fat derived from one or more types of vegetable oil. Do not use low-fat margarines in quick bread baking, since they contain too much added water.

Millet. A small seed of a cereal grass or grain closely related to corn. With a nutty aroma and taste, it is an excellent source of fiber and moderate source of protein.

Mixed glazed fruit. A mixture of dried candied orange and lemon peel, citron and glazed cherries. Citron, which can be expensive, is often replaced in the mix by candied rutabaga.

Molasses. A byproduct of refining sugar, molasses is a sweet, thick, dark-brown (almost black) liquid. It has a distinctive, slightly bitter flavor and is available in fancy and blackstrap varieties. Use the fancy variety for quick breads. Store in the refrigerator if used infrequently.

Oat bran. The outer layer of oat grain. It has a high soluble fiber content, which can help to lower blood cholesterol.

Oats. Confusing in its many variations, the term "oats" generally refers to the cereal grass of the oat grain. When the oat husk has been removed, it is called a groat. Oats are steamed and rolled into flat flakes called rolled oats or old-fashioned oats. When coarsely ground oats are cooked and used for baking, it becomes oatmeal. "Instant" oats are partially cooked and dried before rolling. They are rolled thinner, cut finer, and may have flavoring ingredients added. They are not recommended for use in bread machines. "Quick-cooking" oats are rolled oats that are cut into smaller pieces to reduce the cooking time. For a traditional oat bread texture, use small- or medium-flake oatmeal, but not the "instant cooking" type.

Olives (Kalamata). A large, flavorful variety of Greek olive, typically dark purple in color, and pointed at one end. They are usually sold packed in olive oil or vinegar.

Olive oil. Produced from pressing tree-ripened olives. *Extra virgin oil* is taken from the first cold pressing; it is the finest and fruitiest, pale straw to pale green in color with the least amount of acid, usually less than 1%. *Virgin oil* is taken from a subsequent pressing; it contains 2% acid and is pale yellow. *Light oil* comes from the last pressing; it has a mild flavor, light color and up to 3% acid. It also has a higher smoke point. Product sold as "pure olive oil" has been cleaned and filtered; it is very mild-flavored and has up to 3% acid.

Parsley. A biennial herb with dark green, curly or flat leaves used fresh as a flavoring or garnish. It is also used dried in soups and other mixes. Substitute parsley for half the amount of a strong-flavored herb such as basil.

Pecan. The nut of the hickory tree, pecans have a reddish, mahogany shell and beige flesh. They have a high fat content and are a milder-flavored alternative to walnuts.

Peel (mixed, candied or glazed). This type of peel is crystallized in sugar.

Pine nuts. The nuts of various pine trees native to China, Italy, Mexico, North Africa and southwestern United States. A shell covers the ivory-colored meat, which is very rich tasting and high in fat. There are two principal types of pine nut – one mild and long-shaped, the other stronger-flavored and more triangular in shape. Substitute for any variety of nut in quick bread recipes.

Pistachio. Inside a hard, tan-colored shell, this pale green nut has a waxy texture and mild flavor.

Poppy seeds. The tiny, round, blue-gray seed of the poppy has a sweet, nutty flavor. Often used as a garnish or topping for a variety of breads.

Potato flour. See Potato starch.

Potato starch. This very fine powder is a pure starch made from cooked, dried, ground potatoes. It is gluten-free and produces a moist crumb in baked goods. Potato flour, while similar in appearance and also made from potatoes, is a different product and can not be substituted for potato starch.

Pumpkin seeds. Hulled and roasted pumpkin seeds have a nutty flavor that enhances many breads. In Mexico, they are also known as *pepitas*, where they are eaten as a snack and used as a thickener in cooking.

Rhubarb. A perennial plant with long, thin, red- to pink-colored stalks, resembling celery, and large green leaves. Only the tart-flavored stalks are used for cooking, since the leaves are poisonous. For 2 cups (500 mL) cooked rhubarb, you will need 3 cups (750 mL) chopped fresh (about 1 lb [500 g]).

Raisins. Dark raisins are sun-dried Thompson seedless grapes. Golden raisins are treated with sulphur dioxide and dried artificially, yielding a moister, plumper product.

Red River cereal. Originating in the Red River Valley (in Manitoba, Canada), its nutty flavor and chewy texture comes from the combination of cracked wheat, rye and flaxseed.

Rice flour. A fine, powdery-textured flour, gluten-free, made from white or brown rice.

Rye flour. Milled from rye, a cereal grain similar to wheat, this flour can be dark or light in color. Because of its low gluten content, it is always used in combination with wheat flour in bread machine recipes.

Rye groat. A rye kernel that has had its husk removed.

Self-rising flour. All-purpose white wheat flour to which salt and baking powder have been added.

Semolina flour. A creamy-yellow, coarsely ground flour milled from hard Durum wheat. It has a high gluten content. Semolina is used either alone or in combination with all-purpose or bread flour to make pasta. The semolina makes it easier to knead and hold its shape during cooking. Sprinkled on a baking sheet, it gives a crunch to Kaisers, French sticks and focaccia.

Sesame seeds. Small, flat, oval-shaped seeds with a rich, nut-like flavor when roasted. Purchase the tan (hulled), not black (unhulled) variety for use in a quick bread.

Shortening. A partially hydrogenated fat made from either animal or vegetable sources.

Skim milk powder. The dehydrated form of fluid skim milk. Use 1/4 cup (50 mL) skim milk powder for every 1 cup (250 mL) water.

Sorghum flour. Also known as Juwar. A grass cultivated as a grain, a relative of millet, used for flour in Middle East, Africa and Northern China. It has a nutty flavor that produces a nicely browned crust and a flavor similar to wheat. It is gluten-free.

Sour cream. A thick, smooth, tangy-flavored product made by adding bacterial cultures to pasteurized, homogenized cream containing varying amounts of butterfat.

Soy flour. Coarser in texture and stronger flavored than soya flour. Gluten-free and not very pleasant tasting, it must be used in combination with other flours.

Soya flour. Made from toasted soybeans, high in fat and protein. This low-fat flour is milled from raw beans.

Sugar substitute. For baking, the best choice is sucralose, which is made from processed sugar, and remains stable at any temperature.

Sun-dried tomatoes. Available either dry or oil-packed, sun-dried tomatoes have a dark red color, soft, chewy texture and strong tomato flavor. Use either dry-packed, or soft sun-dried tomatoes in quick bread recipes. Use scissors to snip the soft dry tomatoes into pieces.

Sunflower oil. A pale-yellow, flavorless oil, high in polyunsaturated fats and low in saturated fats.

Sunflower seeds. Use shelled, unsalted, unroasted sunflower seeds in quick bread recipes. If only roasted, salted seeds are available, rinse under hot water and dry well before using.

Sweet potato. A tuber with orange flesh that stays moist when cooked. Not the same as a yam, although yams can substitute for sweet potatoes in quick bread recipes.

Tapioca. A granular, starchy food prepared from cassava (the edible root of a tropical plant), used as a thickening agent. It is a white, slightly sweet powder which thickens as it cools.

Tapioca starch. Produced from the root of cassava plant, this starch is used for thickening. Tapioca flour can be substituted. To substitute for cornstarch, use 2 tbsp (25 mL) tapioca starch for 1 tbsp (15 mL) cornstarch.

Tarragon. A herb with narrow, pointed, dark green leaves and a distinctive anise-like flavor with undertones of sage. Use fresh or dried.

Unbleached flour. Gives loaves a creamier color; may be used interchangeably with bleached, all-purpose or bread flour.

Vegetable oil. Common oils used are corn, sunflower, safflower, olive, canola, peanut and soya.

Walnuts. A sweet-fleshed nut with a large, wrinkled shell.

Wheat berry. The berry is the whole wheat kernel which includes the endosperm, bran and germ.

Wheat bran. The outer layer of the wheat berry or kernel, high in fiber and used as a cereal. Oat bran can be substituted in equal amounts.

Wheat germ. The embryo of the wheat berry, wheat germ has a nutty flavor, crunchy texture and is rich in vitamins (particularly vitamin E) and minerals. It is oily and must be kept in the refrigerator to prevent it becoming rancid. Wheat germ cannot be substituted for wheat bran.

White flour. A flour made by finely grinding the wheat kernel and separating out the germ and bran. It is enriched with vitamins (thiamin, niacin, riboflavin, folic acid) and minerals (iron).

Whole-wheat flour. A flour made by grinding the entire wheat berry – the bran, germ and endosperm. Store in freezer to keep fresh.

Wild rice. Native to North America, this nutty-flavored seed does not come from a rice plant, but from a type of grass.

Xanthan gum. A gum produced from the fermentation of glucose used to modify texture. Used as an ingredient in gluten-free quick breads to give the dough strength, thus allowing it to rise and prevent it from being too dense in texture. It does not mix with water, so must be combined with dry ingredients. Purchase from bulk or health-food stores.

Yeast. A tiny, single-celled organism that, given moisture, food and warmth, creates gas that is trapped in bread dough, causing it to rise.

Yogurt. Made by fermenting cows' milk using a bacteria culture. Choose unflavored for quick bread recipes.

Zest. Strips from the outer layer of rind of citrus fruit. Used for its intense flavor.

Almonds. *To blanch:* Cover almonds with boiling water and allow to stand, covered, for 3 to 5 minutes; drain. Grasp the almond at one end, pressing between your thumb and index finger and the nut will pop out of the skin. Nuts are more easily chopped or slivered while still warm from blanching. *To toast:* see Nuts.

Baking pan. *To prepare:* Either spray the bottom and sides of the baking pan with a nonstick cooking spray or brush with a pastry brush dipped in vegetable oil or a crumpled up piece of waxed paper.

Bananas. *To mash and freeze:* Select overripe fruit, mash and package in 1-cup (250 mL) amounts in freezer containers. Freeze for up to 6 months. Defrost and warm to room temperature before using.

Beat. Stir vigorously to incorporate air using a spoon, whisk, hand-beater or electric mixer.

Blend. Mix two or more ingredients together thoroughly, with a spoon or using the low speed of an electric mixer.

Caramelize onions. See Onions.

Chocolate. *To melt:* Foods high in fat (such as chocolate) soften and then become a liquid when heated. Microwave on High for 1 minute per 1-oz (30 g) square.

Coconut. *To toast:* See Oats.

Combine. Stir two or more ingredients together for a consistent mixture.

Cream. Ttechnique of combining softened fat and sugar by beating to a soft, smooth, creamy, consistency while trying to incorporate as much air as possible.

Cream cheese. *To warm to room temperature:* For each 8-oz (250 g) pkg; cut into 1-inch (2.5 cm) cubes, arrange in a circle on a microwave-safe plate and microwave on High for 1 minute.

Crêpes. *To store:* For the short term, wrap stacked crêpes in foil or plastic wrap and refrigerate for 2 to 3 days. For long-term storage, separate crêpes with waxed paper and put in airtight container. Freeze for up to 4 months. Handle frozen crêpes carefully, since they are very fragile. Thaw before filling. *To test pan temperature:* Drops of water should sizzle upon contact with pan.

Cut in. Technique used for combining cold, solid fat and flour until the fat is the size required (for example, like small peas or meal). Use either two knives or a pastry blender.

Drizzle. Slowly spoon or pour a liquid (such as icing or melted butter) in a very fine stream over the surface of food.

Dust. Coat by sprinkling icing sugar, cocoa or flour lightly over food or a utensil.

Eggs. *To warm to room temperature:* Place eggs in the shell from the refrigerator in a bowl of hot water and allow to stand for 5 minutes.

Flaxseed. *To grind:* Place whole seeds in a coffee grinder or blender. Grind only the amount required. If necessary, store extra ground flaxseed in refrigerator.

Fold. Gently combine light whipped ingredients with heavier without losing the incorporated air. Using a rubber spatula, gently fold in a circular motion; move down one side of the bowl and across the bottom, fold up and over to the opposite side and down again turning bowl slightly after each fold.

Glaze. Apply a thin, shiny coating to the outside of a baked, sweet or savory food to enhance the appearance and flavor

Grease pan. See Baking pan.

Griddle. *To test for correct temperature:* Sprinkle a few drops of water on the surface. If the water bounces and dances across the pan, it is ready to use.

Hazelnuts. *To remove skins:* Place hazelnuts in a 350° F (180° C) oven for 15 to 20 minutes. Immediately place in a clean, dry kitchen towel. With your hands, rub the nuts against the towel. Skins will be left in the towel. Be careful: hazelnuts will be very hot.

Herbs. *To clean fresh leaves:* Rinse under cold running water and spin-dry in a lettuce spinner. If necessary, dry between layers of paper towels. Place a dry paper towel along with the clean herbs in a plastic bag in the refrigerator for short-term storage. Freeze or dry for longer storage. *To dry:* Tie fresh-picked herbs together in small bunches and hang upside down in a well-ventilated location with low humidity until the leaves are brittle and fully dry. If they turn brown (rather than stay green), the air is too hot. Once fully dried, strip leaves off the stems for storage. Store whole dried herbs in an airtight container in a cool dark place for 1 year and dried crushed herbs for 6 months. Dried herbs are stored in the dark to prevent the color from fading. Check herbs and discard any that have faded, lost flavor or smell old and musty. *To dry using a microwave:* Place 1/2 to 1 cup (125 to 250 mL) of herbs between layers of paper towels. Microwave on High for 3 minutes, checking often to be sure they are not scorched. Microwave for extra15-second periods until leaves are brittle and can be pulled from stems easily. *To freeze:* Lay whole herbs in a single layer on a flat surface in the freezer for 2 to 4 hours, leave whole and pack in plastic bags. Crumble the leaves directly into the dish. Leaves of herbs are also easier to chop when frozen. Use frozen leaves only for flavoring and not garnishing as they loose their crispness when thawed. Some herbs such as chives have a very weak flavor when dried and do not freeze well but they do grow well inside on a window sill. *To measure:* Remove small leaves from stem by holding the top and running fingers down the stem in the opposite direction of growth. Larger leaves should be snipped off the stem using scissors. Pack leaves tightly into correct measure. *To snip:* After measuring, transfer to a small glass and cut using the tips of sharp kitchen shears/scissors to prevent bruising the tender leaves. *To store:* Fresh picked herbs can be stored for up to 1 week with stems standing in water. (Keep leaves out of water.)

Juice. *To warm to room temperature:* See Milk.

Knead. Work with a dough to develop gluten. On a lightly floured surface, gather dough pieces together, fold dough over on itself. Push away from you with the heels of your hands. Turn dough a quarter turn and repeat the fold, push and turn operation. Flour hands before beginning and keep extra flour handy to use as dough begins to stick to kneading surface.

Milk. *To warm to room temperature:* For each 1 cup (250 mL) refrigerated liquid, microwave on High for 1 minute.
To sour: Add 1 tbsp (15 mL) lemon juice or vinegar to 1 cup (250 mL) of milk. Stir.

Millet. *To cook:* Similar to rice, add 1 cup (250 mL) millet to 3 cups (750 mL) boiling water and simmer 20 minutes to yield 3 1/2 cups (875 mL) cooked.

Mix. Combine two or more ingredients uniformly by stirring or with an electric mixer on a low speed.

Nuts. *To toast:* Spread nuts in a single layer on a baking sheet and bake at 350° F (180° C) for about 10 minutes, shaking the pan frequently, until lightly browned. (Or microwave uncovered on High for 1 to 2 minutes, stirring every 30 seconds.) Nuts will darken upon cooling.

Oats. *To toast:* Spread rolled oats in a shallow pan. Bake at 350° F (180° C) for 10 to 15 minutes or until brown; stir often. Store in an airtight container or freeze.

Olives. *To pit:* Place olives under the flat side of a large knife; push down on knife until pit pops out.

Onions. *To caramelize:* In a nonstick frying pan, heat 1 tbsp (15 mL) oil over medium heat. Add 2 cups (500 mL) sliced or chopped onions; cook slowly until soft and caramel-colored. If necessary, add 1 tbsp (15 mL) water or white wine to prevent sticking while cooking.

Raisins. *To plump:* Measure spirit (usually brandy) into liquid measuring cup and add raisins; microwave on High for 1 minute and allow to cool.

Sauté. Cook quickly in a small amount of fat at high temperature.

Sour milk. See Milk, to sour.

Sesame seeds. *To toast:* See Sunflower seeds.

Springform pan. *How to remove cake from:* Remove pan from oven and cool on a wire rack for 10 minutes. Using a spatula or kitchen knife, trace around the edge between the pan and cake before removing the side by opening the clip on the side.

Sunflower seeds. *To toast:* Spread seeds in a single layer on a baking sheet and bake at 350° F (180° C) for 10 minutes, shaking pan frequently, until lightly browned. (Or microwave uncovered on High for 1 to 2 minutes, stirring every 30 seconds.) Seeds will darken upon cooling.

Waffle iron. *To test for correct temperature:* If no indicator light, pour a drop of water on cooking surface; if water boils and forms a small ball, it is ready to use. If it sizzles, it is too hot. Alternatively, put a teaspoon of water on iron, close it and when steam stops, it is ready to use.

Yogurt. *To warm to room temperature:* For each 1 cup (250 mL), microwave on Medium for 2 minutes, stirring once.

Wheat berry. *To cook:* In a bowl cover wheat berry with at least 1 inch (2.5 cm) water; let stand overnight. Drain. Add fresh water to cover. Transfer to a pot over medium heat. Simmer, stirring occasionally, for 30 to 45 minutes or until tender. Drain and allow to cool before using. Store in refrigerator.

Wheat germ. *To toast:* Spread wheat germ in a single layer on a baking sheet and bake at 350° F (180° C) for about 3 to 4 minutes, shaking the pan frequently, until lightly browned. (Or microwave uncovered on High for 30 to 90 seconds, stirring every 30 seconds.) Wheat germ will darken upon cooling.

Whip. Beat ingredients vigorously to increase volume and incorporate air, typically using a fork, whisk or electric mixer. *Whip eggs to soft peaks:* Egg whites beaten to a foam that comes up as the beaters are lifted and fold over at the tips. *Whip eggs to stiff peaks:* Egg whites beaten past soft peaks until the peaks remain upright when the beaters are lifted.

Wild rice. *To cook:* Rinse 1/3 cup (75 mL) wild rice under cold running water. Add along with 3 1/3 cups (825 mL) water to a large saucepan. Bring to a boil and cook uncovered at a gentle boil for about 35 minutes. Reduce heat, cover and cook for 10 minutes or until rice is soft but not mushy. Makes 1 cup (250 mL). Store in refrigerator.

Zest. *To zest:* Use a zester or small sharp knife to peel off thin strips of the colored part of the skin. Be sure not to remove the bitter white pith below.

L

Lemon
  blueberry almond bread, 113
  coconut bread, 105
  glaze, 105, 172
  loaf, 172
    from a mix, 152
  poppy seed quick bread, 159
  sauce, 78–79
  sunshine loaf from a mix, 163
  yogurt biscuits, 166
Lime
  glaze, 172
  loaf, 172
Low-fat breads, 117–26

M

Macadamia nuts
  chocolate bread, 106
  chocolate drop biscuits, 65
Maraschino cherry loaf, 173
Maritime molasses date bran loaf, 31
Mediterranean loaf, 32
Millet, orange loaf, 123
Mixes
  multigrain pancake and waffle, 92
  pancake and waffle, 92
  quick bread, 141
Mock Christmas cake, 26
Molasses, date bran loaf, 31
Morning glory bread, 107
Mother's banana bread, 168
Multigrain
  banana loaf, 118
  pancake and waffle mix, 92
  waffles, 96

N

Nutmeg sour cream bread, 108
Nut(s)
  baking tips, 38
  pancakes, 95
  See also specific nuts

O

Oats
  apple raisin loaf from a mix, 151
  blueberry
    banana bread, 101
  poppy seed bread, 46
  scones, 34
Onions
  caramelized vidalias, 60–61
  cutting tip, 60–61
Orange
  apricot bread, 100
  buttermilk chocolate loaf, 102
  carrot date loaf from a mix, 160
  chocolate waffles, 89
  date bread, 121
  date loaf from a mix, 150
  millet loaf, 123
  nutty mocha loaf, 109
  poppy seed quick bread, 159
  pumpkin snacking cake, 80
  rhubarb bread, 22
  sauce, 90–91
  streusel loaf, 110
  sunshine loaf from a mix, 163
  tutti-fruiti loaf, 164
Ovens, temperatures of, 9

P

Pancake and waffle mix, 92
Pancakes
  applesauce, 93
  banana blueberry, 94
  multigrain nut, 95
  tips, 84
  yeast-raised, Russian blini, 33
Parmesan walnut bread, 42
Peach
  blueberry quick bread, 23
  pinwheel brunch cake, 81
Peanut butter crunch loaf, 43

All the best for your bread machine!

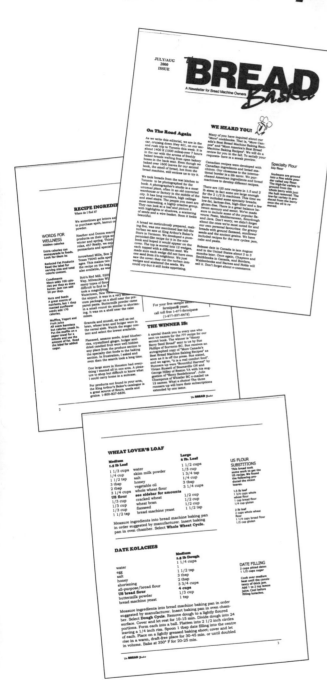

If you love baking with your bread machine, then you should subscribe to Donna and Heather's newsletter, *The Bread Basket*. Published by Quality Professional Services (QPS) and written specially for bread machine owners, this bimonthly publication features 12 pages of useful information, including:

- Seven previously unpublished bread machine recipes – with quantities for both 1.5 and 2 lb machines (even some for 1 lb and 2.5 lb models) – from the QPS test kitchen

- Tips on buying and using different types of flours, grains and other ingredients

- What you need to know about the features of various bread machines in order to make an informed purchase decision

- Answers to readers' questions

- And much, much more...

Annual subscriptions are only US$16 in the USA or C$17.65 in Canada (GST included). (In the maritime provinces, the cost is C$18.98, HST included.) To start your subscription, send a cheque, payable to Quality Professional Services, to the appropriate address below.

In the USA:
QPS
P. O. Box 1382
Ogdensburg, NY 13669

In Canada:
QPS
1655 County Rd #2
Mallorytown, ON
K0E 1R0

**For more information, call
(613) 923-2116
or visit our website at
www.bestbreadrecipes.com**

Be sure to include your name, address and zip or postal code.